Redundant

Redundant
An emotional and spiritual journey through Redundancy
By Brian Keith
ISBN: 978-0-9926563-9-3

www.briankeithbooks.co.uk

Redundant
An emotional and spiritual journey through Redundancy
By Brian Keith
ISBN: 978-0-9926563-9-3

Published by

i2i Publishing. Manchester.
www.i2ipublishing.co.uk

For Tanya
It is simply impossible to imagine the journey without you

Redundant/adjective.

Plentiful, copious, abundant, full.

Superfluous, excessive, unnecessary; having some additional or unneeded feature or part

Shorter Oxford English Dictionary, 6th Edition

Author's Note:
This book is inspired by true events and is an accurate depiction of what occurred to me but names and identities have been changed to preserve anonymity where appropriate.

CONTENTS

Preface

On the morning of December 5th, 2013, the entire world woke up to an almost identical headline; *Nelson Mandela Dead*. Although I never met him personally, I vividly remember the first time that one of history's truly extraordinary leaders significantly impacted my life. I was nineteen years old; it was the 11th of February, 1990....

In the prehistoric era of no internet and giant mobile phones, if you had not seen a newspaper or watched the TV for a few days, you didn't know much about what was going on the in the world. Having just returned to the big city after spending five glorious days in the isolation of South Africa's remote Kruger National Park, I was startled by what I witnessed as I turned into Fox Street, one of downtown Johannesburg's main arteries. Thousands of people were dancing down the middle of the road, heading straight in my direction. And this was no ordinary dance; it was the Toyi-Toyi, the traditional mass protest march of South Africa's oppressed black majority. I had only ever seen the Toyi-Toyi on TV and it always appeared to be associated with violence and chaos (or at least that was what the government-controlled media led us to believe). To me, the sight of those dancing, marching throngs spelled only one thing; trouble.

Sliding my car into reverse, I sped quickly backwards up the road, aiming to put as much distance as possible between myself and the unruly masses. I turned into Commissioner Street, gripping the steering wheel hard with tension. What was going on? Was a revolution about to occur? Had the country descended into disorderly chaos in the few days I had been away? I was bewildered and scared. And then, pulling up at a traffic-light, a newspaper headline sprawled across a placard caught the corner of my eye; *Mandela Freed Today.*

Instantly, all became clear. I had not witnessed a protest march aimed at overthrowing the government. The country was not imploding. It was rejoicing. The Toyi-Toyi was a dance of celebration. After 27 years in prison, Madiba had been freed, and, what, only moments ago, had seemed to be a scenario so frightening to me could not have been further from the truth. In that moment, I experienced the most extreme transformation. Feelings of fear and despair were replaced with optimism and joy. Neither myself, nor the rest of the country, knew exactly what the future heralded. But the next stage of our nation's journey had suddenly been filled with hope.

Twenty-three years later, I would come face-to-face with another moment of sudden transformation. This time, the only real impact would be on my family and me. Had I learnt the lesson that Nelson Mandela's release taught me when I was nineteen years old? Could I – would I – come to understand that what seemed to be one thing was indeed something very different?

Nothing could be more important than how I answered that question. And that answer, and how I arrived at it, is what this book about.

Redundancy is almost a dirty word for many people. I know – it was for me.

In organisational terms, redundancy is often used as a euphemism for getting rid of someone. Some associated terms; severance, laid off. Worse still; fired, retrenched, sacked. By the beginning of 2013, almost four million people in the UK had been made redundant since the onset of the Global Financial Crisis. And I suspect that almost every person, myself included, who makes up that staggering statistic, can relate to the pejorative associations implicit in the word redundant. Simply put, we are part of a club, that though almost as common numerically as the number of dog owners in the UK, we do not like belonging to.

Yet a brief consultation with the Oxford English Dictionary revealed a fascinating, scarcely believable paradox. The word redundant actually has two distinctly opposite meanings; superfluous and abundant. This, then, became the contradiction to address and resolve. What did redundant really mean to me? How should I feel – superfluous or abundant?

I started writing this book the day after I was made redundant from the job I had held in a top tier City bank for six years, so there's no question that I had become superfluous. And I'm no longer talking only in a work sense. I'm talking about how I, Brian Keith - husband, father, human being, spiritual entity – had become redundant. And that meant I had to ask myself some tough questions. The kind of questions I had avoided asking for a long time. Had I lost touch with myself? Had I become superfluous? Had I been dismissed, severed, sacked? Not by another, but by myself?

This was the point to which the formal redundancy had brought me. And as the dictionary definition implied, I needed to ask myself further; could I find my way back to abundance? Could I make the experience of redundancy mean something completely different for me?

And the experience of redundancy, my experience, is what this book is about. At its heart is a different approach to most books I have encountered on the subject, which typically fall into one of two broad categories; either a practically-oriented 'how to guide' of managing the redundancy process from a legal and procedural perspective; or a motivational handbook aimed at bouncing back into work as effortlessly as possible.

My approach differs markedly, for I have aimed to describe the effect on my inner self of being made redundant, and more importantly, the impact it has had on my life. I have used the experience of being made redundant to look deeply inside myself, and in so doing, have arrived at insights and understandings that have profoundly changed my life. I have sought to express how I felt – less than what I did – and it is the exploration of these feelings, and where they led me - psychologically, emotionally and spiritually - that is the leitmotif of this book. This is a story about finding the inner authentic self, the one that has been obscured and hidden beneath layers of self-image so thick that the self and the image seem to merge into a singular, indivisible illusion. It is about finding humility, and by extension, perspective. It is about finding understanding - the deep understanding of self that provides the opportunity for so much illumination and liberation. And it is about how I found myself again, after having been lost for quite some time.

As I am not a celebrity, a reformed criminal or a person who has experienced an exceptionally traumatic life, my story is quite ordinary - it's just about me and what I've learned. Yet I am emboldened by the recommendation of the ethical teachers of my tradition who advise every person to record their own life events. The rationale, as I understand it, is that by reflecting on one's own life experiences, a person will hopefully come to develop greater insight and self-understanding. This, I have discovered, helps to build perspective and encourages self-development, and, with the right intent, leads to spiritual growth and the nurturing of faith.

You don't have to have been made redundant to benefit from this book. You just need to be someone who has asked, or is willing to ask, similar questions to the ones that I asked myself. Of course, I do not presume to have all the answers - perhaps not any of them. All I have is my experiences, my insights, and what I have learned. And though the questions I pose are deeply personal, I believe they are also universal. They are questions about us, about humanity.

I

The Self Image Illusion

In the direction a person wishes to go, they will be led
The Talmud

.

1. I've lost myself somehow

When a man is pushed, tormented, defeated, he has a chance to learn something.
Ralph Waldo Emerson

May 22nd 2013
Room 105 on the first floor.
Over the last few years, I had spent more hours in that room than any other in the building that housed SKBK Bank in the heart of the City of London. It sometimes felt as if I spent more time in 105 than in my own bedroom. This was the 'Exec' room, the one in which our ten person Executive Committee, myself included, had met exactly a week earlier to hear about my boss, Tony's sudden and completely unexpected retirement and immediate resignation.

With its long rectangular conference table, comfy chairs and floor to ceiling windows, Room 105 was the perfect place to hold all important meetings for Investment and Commercial Banking, the 1,000 person division that Tony had headed and which I served as Head of Strategic and Business Development. It was also the venue for our Deal Committee, a regular meeting held every Monday and Wednesday from 11;00 – 13;00 when all transactions the division was considering were scrutinised by the senior business heads. I was deputy Chair of that Committee and ran the meeting on Tony's behalf. Room 105 was my theatre of operation, the place where I displayed my wares and excelled at my game. It was my home pitch and my comfort zone.

But that was all about to change. I had been invited to a meeting with Craig Hertford who just been promoted from being a peer of mine on the Executive Committee to being appointed the new head of the division. In other words, Craig, all six foot two, highly polished and well-regarded businessman, had just become my new boss.

"Can I pour you a coffee?" Craig asked as I walked in.

"No, I'm good thanks", I replied as I closed the door behind me. "I'm feeling a bit over-caffeinated for one day," I said, trying not to show my nervousness.

We sat down at the table and I crossed my legs. "I guess with the new appointment that you've had a ton going on the last few days," I commented. That's me – Mr. Emotionally Intelligent and king of the ice-breaker.

"Man, you've got no idea", Craig responded with a shake of his head.

He paused and glanced at the door a little awkwardly. The silence lasted another second or so and I felt a small bead of sweat form at the back of my neck. I waited for him to say more and wondered what was holding him back. Something was up. Then I heard the door handle turn and looked to my right. Standing there was the tall, lithe frame of Lauren from HR, holding an A4 envelope and looking a little uncomfortable. She hadn't been on the original invitation for this meeting – at least not the version I had received.

"Come in Lauren", Craig said. And as she crossed the threshold into Room 105, everything came sharply into focus. I had been expecting a conversation reviewing what I was involved with and the redefining of our strategic priorities under the new leadership, but now I suddenly became acutely aware of what Lauren was doing there. The envelope in her hand was for me.

Everything seemed to slow down as my mind grappled with accepting what was about to occur. Tony had seen me as his 'go-to guy'; he had gone so far as to create this role specifically so as to have someone he trusted who could execute specific projects and initiatives on his behalf. That someone was me. But Craig wasn't Tony and therein lay my problem. He was at a completely different stage of his career and looking to be much more of a hands-on leader; having a guy like me as a kind of a middle man didn't really work for him. Add to that the fact that Craig didn't particularly like Tony and you didn't need to be a rocket scientist to work out that there was about to be some collateral damage resulting from Tony's departure – and I was it! My horse had bolted the stable and I was left holding the reins. In that moment, as this all became abundantly clear to me, I'm not sure if I've ever felt so desperately helpless. Sitting in that room with Craig and Lauren and that piece of paper inside that envelope, there was not a single thing I could do to change what was about to happen to my life.

Lauren gave Craig an almost imperceptible nod and the new boss cleared his throat.

"Brian, you know how much I respect you and the work we've done together in the past. We've always got along well and I think you're a great guy." I nodded and had a momentary flash of a very similar conversation when Lisa Buckley broke the news that she was breaking up with me when I was sixteen. The gravity of Craig's tone brought me quickly back from my fleeting teenage reverie.

"But we're going to go in a different direction; do things differently," Craig intoned. "The role you were doing for

Tony just doesn't make sense to me. To be honest, what you were doing for Tony is what I specifically see as my responsibility. I'll need some help but it will be more of an admin-type thing and you're just too over-qualified for that kind of work. So I'm really, really sorry Brian, because you've just been caught right in the middle of something that is not at all of your own making. But I'm going to have to discontinue the role."

And with that, as if part of a perfectly choreographed performance, Lauren deftly pulled a single piece of paper out of the A4 envelope and smoothly slid it across the table to me. It was exactly one typed page and at the top, in bold 14 inch font was the single word that would come to define the current reality of my working life;

Redundancy

The word seemed to be staring straight at me, boring into my soul. Its implications were devastating, and by that I am not referring to the financial and practical consequences – those considerations and fears would come later. I'm talking about something far deeper, almost existential in nature. I'm talking about the grievous sense of loss that this word implied. I'm talking about how I suddenly felt. Once you saw past all the niceties, Craig was in essence telling me one basic fact; I was no longer needed. I had become superfluous.

As the stark reality of that realisation sunk in, an interesting phrase that Tony had liked to use came into my mind; 'inflection point'. Well, as evidenced literally by the black and white words in front of me, my inflection point –

the key moment when a critical decision needed to be made - had arrived.

Now you might be wondering what I mean, for there was clearly no decision that required making. The decision had been made already, and I had not been consulted. I was being made redundant. It was as simple as that. The book had already been written, and in this case, it consisted of a single A4 page.

But of course that's only one side of the story – the side which I had no capacity to change. And even though I didn't fully realise it yet, an almost infinite array of critical decisions – emotional, psychological, spiritual and practical – were confronting me at that very moment. How I responded to them was entirely within my own hands.

Another story was just unfolding, and that as yet unwritten story had only one author. And I guess that's the story that I want to tell here.

The house had finally gone quiet. When you've got six sons, three of whom are teenagers, you get used to your home resembling a surreal blend of Wembley Stadium, the Olympic Velodrome and a professional wrestling ring. But by 10;32 pm on the first official night of my redundancy, the inmates had finally turned themselves in and the asylum was at last settling down for the night.

My wife Tanya and I were lying next to each other on our backs on our large bed, looking up at the ceiling of our loft bedroom. Since the meeting with Craig and Lauren had ended almost seven hours earlier, this was our first chance to discuss the big news.

"So, how are you feeling?" Tanya enquired gently.

"Um, not too bad Sweetie", I started. "I mean, they were all quite nice about it, and you know, it wasn't that unexpected really since Tony left. I had kind of warned you that something like this could happen." I took a deep breath and was about to continue with the spin when my voice seemed to catch in my throat.

"I, I .... I think ...."

And then it hit me, like a wave crashing onto the shore with devastating ferocity. I began to cry. Not just cry but really, really weep. Tears came gushing out of me with a crushing intensity. I hadn't cried like that since my father had died seventeen years ago. Something felt like it had broken inside of me; the grief was overwhelming. The hurt, the fear, the pain, the desperation – these feelings were as visceral as any I could remember. I was stunned by how overpowering my sorrow was. For a long while, I couldn't speak. We just lay there, Tanya holding me tight and stroking my hair.

Finally, as the sobs subsided, I began to talk, trying to make sense of this deep sadness I was feeling. "I feel I've lost my way over these last six years," I began. Tanya just listened, her eyes full of softness, compassion and most revealing to me – understanding.

"I mean sure, at one level it's been a big success. You know that. But deep, deep down, something else has happened. I've lost myself somehow; I've neglected the stuff that really matters to me. You know me Sweetie. I'm a soft, gentle person. But the kids barely see that soft side of me now; you don't get enough of that from me. I feel like I've become hard - hard on the outside."

I paused, struggling to articulate the overwhelming feelings that had brought me to this moment of intense self-honesty.

"And I've become so caught up in myself – so preoccupied with my own success. This isn't what we set out to achieve in our lives. This stuff never mattered so much to us, but it does to me now. Where has my gentleness gone? What's happened to the sweet, caring guy I used to be? I feel so sad, so embarrassed about what I've let happen to me ..."

I couldn't finish my sentence. Another heart-wrenching sob escaped, my body shuddering with the profound sorrow I was feeling. I wept deeply and uncontrollably, crying for all of me which I felt had been lost.

Finally, after what seemed the longest time, I continued. "I know you've been trying to tell me this for so long; I know that's why you've been upset with me at times, pushed me to speak to someone, asked me to reconsider where this was all heading. But I've been so stubborn, so caught up in myself. I've pursued this job and my success relentlessly – now look where I've ended up? All its done is alienated you and the kids. I'm so, so sorry."

There was nothing left to say. And so - my eyes red, my heart sore, my soul anguished - I finally stopped speaking.

Shifting her body on the bed, Tanya turned to face me. She didn't need to respond or say anything. She knew exactly what I meant; she had been by my side through it all. As I gazed at my wife through tear-stained eyes, I was overcome with the same feelings of love, warmth and deep security that always overwhelm me when I stop to reflect on what she means to me. With her long, brown hair splayed onto the white pillow, her face emitted deep empathy and concern, which did not obscure her strikingly feminine features; soft, green eyes, high cheekbones, a dark complexion and a slender, delicate figure. There is almost a physical vulnerability to Tanya – she barely weighs eight stone in her trainers - that belies an immense inner strength and causes most people to react in shock when they discover that she is the mother of six children. And as my eyes searched hers, I felt a deep reassurance. After nineteen years of marriage, having spent almost our entire adult lives together and having shared many more of life's never ending vicissitudes, we were facing one of those BIG life moments. And Tanya was right there with me. Not just in a physical sense, nor even an emotional one. The sense of oneness was far more transcendent. I didn't need to explain what was going on inside of me, and she didn't need an explanation. Of course she knew what I meant when I sobbed about losing my way. Of course she understood my inner pain, which ran far deeper than the relatively superficial layer of rejection and hurt I was feeling. She knew because she had been the one trying to point me in this direction for much of the last six years. She knew because more than anyone else alive, she understood me – my potential, my drives, my dreams, my deep fears, my blind spots, my soul. She knew, because as much as is possible in nearly two decades of loving each other, we had become one.

It would be a cliché to say I cried myself to sleep that night. It would even be inaccurate to say I cried myself out – there would be more tears to come in the following days and weeks as the carefully crafted self-image I had constructed underwent some serious renovations. But it would not be a stretch to say that my weeping that night was the catalyst for my catharsis. Something deep within me had shifted. Together with my extraordinary wife, I was ready to start authoring a different story about my redundancy; a story where the term 'redundant' was imbued with connotations of 'plentiful, copious, abundant, full.' I didn't yet know the ending to that story, but I knew clearly that I had arrived at a different version of its beginning.

2. Mind the gap

Life can only be understood backwards, but it must be lived forwards.
Soren Kierkegaard

So how had we come to this moment? How had I lost my way so badly?

Maybe the best place to start is when I met the only woman I've ever loved. (Sorry Mom, but you know what I mean). I know that sounds a bit trite, but it's actually true.

It was in Johannesburg, South Africa, where we both grew up in the relative comfort of the city's Northern Suburb's Jewish community. I was 23; Tanya had just turned 20. Our paths had crossed a couple of times before – and though I fell for her hard (what can I say, I was a pretty shallow guy at the time) – I had been unable to muster up the courage to say anything more intelligible than; "Nice weather we've been having lately, don't you think?" In the local community at the time, she seemed to be the girl every guy wanted to go out with. I was an average looking fellow, a bit on the vertically challenged side but with enough personality and charisma, blueish-green eyes, Semitic features and dark brown hair to be in with a shout. The problem always arose however when an actual female human being was involved. Somehow, this was frequently accompanied by a dizzying loss of confidence and a predilection for speaking too much about my Jack Russell's obesity whenever the conversation turned more personal.

To those who know me from the football pitch or committee meetings, this might come as a surprise. With other guys and in groups, I was extroverted, confident, bordering on cocky. I could speak in front of large crowds no problem; I engaged my esteemed university professors with ease. At weddings, I was the guy who dressed up unashamedly in a full length chicken-suit outfit and fearlessly juggled raw eggs in front of the deliriously happy bride and groom (or at least that's what I did at my sister and brother-in-law's wedding; my mother seemed to enjoy it). If I wasn't exactly the life of the party, I was certainly one its major contributors. But put me one-to-one in a room with a girl, never mind a really, really pretty one, and I froze up. I became the shy, awkward guy who had to ask my mother's best friend's daughter to the high school dance because I was too hopeless to arrange a 'proper' date (sadly, that's a true story).

So imagine my terror when a rabbi friend of mine called me up one wintry Thursday afternoon, not long after I had graduated from University, and declared the following; "Brian, I've got a date set up for you on Saturday night with Tanya Rosenberg. Pick her up at 8 pm. Don't be late."

I gripped the receiver tightly and suddenly felt myself going weak at the knees. "But Rabbi Saul," I spluttered nervously, "I haven't been on a date in almost four years; in fact, I've barely spoken to a girl in the last four years. What do I say? What do I talk about?"

"Just be yourself, Bri. That's all. You'll be fine."

The thought of *just being myself* with an attractive person of the opposite gender filled with me with dread, but I had long ago learnt to trust Rabbi Saul. Anyhow, what choice did I have; once a *shidduch* – the Jewish version of a blind date – was set in motion, it was very hard to derail it, unless you could prove you were suffering from some kind of incurable genetic disorder. And when I had calmed down sufficiently to reflect on the proposed date, as well as gradually regain the feeling in my left hand which was still holding the phone in a vice like grip, it became obvious that only a seriously devoted blind Catholic priest would turn down the opportunity to go out with Tanya Rosenberg. She was absolutely stunning; her delicate features and very, very nice personality (note to male readers; you must always emphasise this point) drawing me to her in a way I had never experienced before. In addition to being gorgeous, she was also smart, modest, graceful, spiritual and cool. (Just call me Mr. Smooth.) Her father was a successful businessman. She even supported Manchester United. What more could a guy want?

As there always seemed to be a line of guys queuing up to go out with her, I didn't rate my chances highly. But something remarkable happened on the first date – in spite of myself; I was fine; she really seemed to like me. Chemistry is an over-used term, but something definitely clicked between us instantly. When we discovered that we were both the exact same height and shared the opinion that Sir Alex was the greatest manager in football history, I could sense the stars above aligning themselves. We shared a youthful idealism and a commitment to pursuing our Jewish faith and a spiritual lifestyle. Doing my best to keep my tongue from hanging out every time she flashed that brilliant smile and forgave me for repeatedly asking her opinion regarding my dog's new diet, things progressed quickly, so much so that after our third date, desperate to share something intimate with someone, I took Panky - my aforementioned Jack Russell – for a long walk.

"I need to confide something in you Panky," I blurted out to my dog, "She's the one. I'm going to marry this girl."

I was actually telling my dog about the girl who had stolen my heart and touched my soul. Clearly, I needed to expand my social circle - fast.

In the orthodox Jewish community, when boy meets girl and boy likes girl and (more critically in my case), girl likes boy (and even more critically – girl's parents like boy), things happen quickly. How quickly? Well, put it this way; we met at the end of July, were engaged by the beginning of September, and got married at the end of November - all in the same year. We were virtually kids, we barely knew each other, and we had no discernible plan for making a living, or for creating any semblance of a responsible life. But we were experiencing the beginning of something called love and knew we were right for each other.

So off we went to start the process of building a life together with little more than a super-charged injection of infatuation and idealism to set us on our way. Within a few months we had emigrated from South Africa to Israel to deepen our spiritual commitment, setting ourselves up in a cramped, mouldy, rented flat in an isolated settlement amidst the rolling Judean hills on the outskirts of Jerusalem. Soon, we had immersed ourselves completely in our religious studies and its corresponding culture, so completely different from the one we had left behind in South Africa. Indeed, for two young people trying to find our way in the world therein lay one of the great attractions.

Our new adventure together was imbued with many of the normal ups and downs that lots of couples face as they attempt to make an untested relationship work. In our case, we had to confront homesickness, doubts about this whole marriage thing (in Tanya's mind only, I might add), financial pressures and surviving the suicidal tendencies of Israeli bus drivers who seemed intent on treating the Judean Hills Highway as a Middle Eastern version of the Monte Carlo Grand Prix. These challenges we navigated relatively serenely, though in hindsight, relentlessly building up an unpaid account at the local supermarket was probably not the most responsible way to address our perilous financial situation. All was going reasonably well – especially as we learned to travel by taxi whenever a James Hunt look-alike appeared at the bus stop.

And then we hit our first real crisis – and the wheels threatened to come off. Tanya had been desperate to fall pregnant from the beginning of our marriage, and although it was not a need that I felt as deeply, I too shared the incredible feelings of elation when I came home one evening to hear the wonderful news. We spent the first three months in a state of nervous excitement, keeping the secret to ourselves while the miracle of life began to form inside her body. And then, just as we were preparing to share our delight with family and friends, ominous drops of dark, foreboding blood began to appear. We rushed to the nearest hospital, desperately clinging to the hope that all would be well. It wasn't. In a thick Israeli accent and a tired, detached voice, the doctor informed us that Tanya had miscarried and that a minor surgical procedure would be required to completely clean out the lifeless foetus.

I was shocked and saddened; Tanya was completely distraught and inconsolable. Within days of returning home from the hospital, she plunged into a severe depression, unwilling to speak about the loss, see friends or leave the house. I could barely get her to eat or get out of bed. I was desperately concerned and completely out of my depth; nothing that I had experienced in my hopelessly inadequate first 24 years had prepared me for the deep emotional pain and grief that my young bride was experiencing. Alone and afraid, thousands of miles from the support system we could have counted on to nurture us through this traumatic period, I felt helpless. Still, I tried everything I knew; intense prayers at the Western Wall, advice from a psychotherapist friend, soothing words of comfort and hope. Nothing worked. Tanya only seemed to retreat further into herself – and further away from me.

Our new neighbour Lisa, who lived in the apartment next door, was concerned that Tanya wouldn't return her calls or answer the door. So taking matters into her own hands, Lisa deftly slid out of her third floor bedroom window, shimmied across the narrow ledge that joined our two flats, pressing her body close against the wall to avoid looking down at the fifteen foot drop that would have greeted her had she lost her footing. And before you assume that in a previous career Lisa had been a high wire trapeze artist for Cirque de Soleil, it's important to know (and not just for dramatic effect) that she actually has an acute fear of heights; seriously. So imagine the scene; a young mother of two, suffering from intense acrophobia, clambering up the side of a multi-storey apartment block in her long flowing skirt and breaking into her neighbour's flat. Not exactly the best way to start off a friendship.

Nonetheless, Lisa persisted. Eventually making it to safety, she hauled herself over the wall adjoining the ledge and pried open a window that led onto the bedroom balcony. Gingerly placing one leg before the other, Lisa managed to squeeze herself through the window, arriving unannounced on the bedroom floor.

Tanya was about to scream and call the police to inform them that a modestly dressed religious looking Caucasian woman in her mid-twenties had just broken into our bedroom – presumably to steal her hairspray – when she recognised Lisa's features. Unable to offer anything other than a slightly incongruent, "how did you get in here?" Tanya was left speechless in the face of Lisa's heroic exploits. Grasping the opportunity, her intruder reached out with words of empathy and compassion. A connection between the two of them developed - Tanya's decision not to press charges helped - and the beginnings of a deep friendship took root. It didn't happen overnight (that only occurs in rom-coms) but soon Tanya's mood began to lift, as she arrived at her own understanding of what meaning this experience held for her.

In time, we generated a degree of perspective. We realised that we needed to mourn what had been lost, but together, we also came to see this experience as something that we both, but Tanya in particular, needed to go through. Life was teaching us lessons, and although we were responding quite stubbornly at times, we were doing our best to grow and learn.

Exactly a year after the miscarriage, Tanya gave birth to our first son, Baruch, which means 'blessing' in Hebrew. We were overjoyed and suffused with gratitude. Though we were both still young, if slightly less naive, we were already beginning to understand that the unfathomable cosmic ways of the universe had a remarkable way of making sense in the end. And so our life together began to gather momentum as our relationship – and we as individuals - evolved and matured, and as our young family increased rapidly in size. Within five years, we had added four more sons to the family portrait, and Tanya and I had begun transforming our initial infatuation into something far deeper and more enduring.

The next stage of our life was initiated when, having completed my religious studies, I was recruited by an embryonic educational organisation based in London. A couple of pilot trips and visa applications later and we found ourselves preparing to leave the comforting spirituality and sunny familiarity of Israel by stocking up on umbrellas and Wellingtons. Disembarking at Heathrow one cold, damp February morning, we arrived at our small, rented two-and-a-half bedroom home in Golders Green, short on money, friends and family. But infused with a youthful spirit of commitment to a lifestyle that eschewed material gain and instead focussed on contribution, service and our core values, we found ourselves following our own unique path as a couple and as a family.

Before long, I had immersed myself in the demanding outreach work and adult education which my organisation advanced in the local community, while Tanya set about building our home and settling the kids into school. Yet something was quietly gnawing at me, and over time, that something began to transform into a line of thinking that soon became an irreversible course of direction. By mid-2005, after a number of years working in the not-for-profit sector, I decided I needed a change. I had enjoyed what I had done in this line of work and had found it both meaningful and fulfilling; I was making a contribution and having an impact on people's lives, and, in my own small way, on society as well. But something was missing for me.

As I approached my mid-30s, I started to become convinced that I could do more, that I *should* do more. Not for society, but for myself. It wasn't long before my self-image had shifted into overdrive as I began to envisage the possibilities for my life. This was the beginning of what I came to understand much later as the *self-image illusion*, but at the time, I couldn't see it as such. All I could see was a guy who wanted to change the game – and had the confidence to do just that.

So off I went and got myself an MBA from Cass Business School - #2 in the UK, #3 in Europe, # 10 in the World – or so it said on the coffee mug they gave me the day I enrolled. What followed was two intense years of late nights, hard work and futile attempts to get to grips with quantitative statistics and present value calculations. But the unlikely combination of endless supplies of Red Bull and my wife's unwavering support and sacrifice proved enough to get me over the line. Armed with my new found expertise in all things business and management (at least that's what it now said on my CV), I did what any well-connected, resourceful, intelligent man with a decent network and a great education would do to get a job; I asked my wife for help. She told me to speak to Kevin.

Kevin was Leanne's husband. I didn't know him well, but as Leanne was one of Tanya's close friends, it seemed a good place to start. The fact that Kevin was Global Head of Private Client Banking at SKBK Bank didn't hurt either. The problem was that I didn't know the first thing about banking.

Now you may think I'm being modest, but I really, really didn't know anything about banking; or anything to do with making money for that matter. I had an undergraduate degree in English Literature and a Masters degree in Psychotherapy and Counselling. I had even studied Talmudic philosophy and law for a few years. I had lived in Canada, South Africa, Israel and the UK. I had worked as a safari game ranger, an outreach educator and a therapist. Unbeknown to most, I had even represented Great Britain in Masters (that's a euphemism for old men) football at the Jewish version of the Olympic Games. (Beating Brazil in the quarter-finals will always go down as my finest sporting moment; that the opposition were mainly fat, unfit and over-45 will be conveniently ignored for personal ego reasons.) I had thought up and designed some pretty funky educational and leadership programmes in the community. I was idealistic and aspirationally spiritual, with a decent dose of chutzpah mixed into the package. At the time, I had five kids, two dogs, one wife and could play any sport known to man except lacrosse. (Note to reader; nobody outside of Moose-Jaw, Saskatchewan can play lacrosse.) I was a reasonably interesting guy who had done some unusual things. But a banker – you gotta be kidding!

But Kev wasn't the Global Head of Private Client Banking for nothing. He was a very intelligent man who knew an opportunity – and quickly evaluated its associated risk – when he saw one. Something – probably his wife's constant nagging - made him think it may be worth taking a punt on me, so he arranged an interview with Don Brandeis, the Head of Organisation Effectiveness at SKBK Bank. The genius herein; as the essence of the job was about understanding individual and organisational psychology, it was just about the only role in the bank that you could realistically apply for without knowing anything about financial services.

The other act of genius on his part, wittingly or not, was that I (and I say this unashamedly), am a good interview. If you don't believe that I have many weaknesses, just ask my wife and children. But interviewing has proved a consistent strength since I was accepted a year early into

Pleasant Valley Nursery Playgroup after knocking their socks off on the 'come and meet the teacher' day. So when Kev lined up the interview, I was pretty confident. I just had to remember not to mention anything to do with banking (which wasn't difficult as I had very little to say on the subject), nor my rather militant views on dealing with Somali pirates and Premiership footballers who bite other players, and I figured I had a good shot.

Which I did; two weeks and five interviews later, they decided I was a risk worth taking and offered me the job. I was to be part of a small, bespoke group of internal consultants known as the Organisational Effectiveness – or OE team.   We weren't bankers by any stretch of the imagination; rather, our job was to help the guys who made the real money and led the business to understand all the other pieces that make up organisational systems, team dynamics, and leadership issues which are critical for sustained effectiveness. But we had a mandate from the Executive and were regarded as being a key part of the Bank's culture, if not core to its actual financial performance. It was highly stimulating, challenging work that required me to learn something completely different, rigorously apply my mind, and build relationships and ways of working that would be crucial for the development of my new career.

So armed with the new tie my father-in-law had bought me when he heard I was finally getting a 'real job' at the age of 36, I arrived at Bank Underground Station at 8;53 on Monday morning, September 3rd , 2007. As the tube doors opened and I stepped onto the platform, I, and hundreds of my fellow commuters, simultaneously heard the same warning that had become synonymous with the London Underground; 'Mind the gap.'

Have you ever really thought about what these three, one syllable words mean? I certainly hadn't then, but when I reflect on them now, I am struck by their simple profundity. I was making the significant transition from one career to another; from one way of being to a completely different one. And in one sense, I handled that transition reasonably well. Sure, it took me a few months to integrate into my new environment and stop asking questions like; where do the tellers sit? (This is not a cool question in an Investment Bank). But overall, I adapted well, settling enthusiastically into my new career without many self doubts or regrets.

Yet there was a gap between the two worlds I was straddling, and in my bullish pursuit of achieving the image of myself which I had constructed, I barely noticed it. The gap did indeed need minding, but I couldn't be bothered. There was a new life waiting for me on the other side of Bank Station, and as I scrambled off the train and headed single-mindedly for the escalator, the last thing that I was going to let happen was to be distracted by some paternalistic instruction to 'mind the gap.' I'm not sure if any of the other passengers took notice of those three iconic words, but I certainly didn't. I wish I had.

Unfortunately for me, I would only come to hear that warning almost six years later, in May, 2013. And by then, it was too late.

3. The delusion of vanity

After the game, the King and the Pawn go into the same box
Italian Proverb

May 1st
The crowd roared as the ball travelled at lightning speed, upwards and outwards away from home plate. Thirty thousand pairs of eyes followed its trajectory as it cleared the left field wall, eventually coming to a rest in the near empty seats in the top left corner of the stadium. There was another deafening roar from the home fans as the batter circled the bases, following the two team-mates he had batted in with his colossal, game-winning home run. I looked at the scoreboard; *Toronto Blue Jays 9; Boston Red Sox 6*; bottom of the 8th inning. This one was almost over.

I shifted in my seat to get a view of Joe, head of our Canadian office, and lifting my beer glass, we nodded a silent "cheers" to each other. I stuffed a few crisps in my mouth, took a final bite of my hot dog, wiped the dripping mustard off my face with the back of my hand, and took a couple of big sips of beer until the plastic cup was drained. I sat back in the plush leather seat, buoyed by a strong feeling of contentment. This was just about as good as it got.

I was sitting in one of the luxury corporate hospitality boxes at Toronto's purpose-built Rogers Stadium, home of the city's Major League Baseball franchise. The box was filled with twenty of my colleagues from SKBK Bank - an eclectic mix of a dozen people from our small Toronto and New York offices, plus another eight senior guys from our head office in London. Tonight's ball game was the chance to bond and enjoy ourselves. It was the culmination of two days of intensive meetings during which we had explored, probed and strategised how we could expand our rapidly growing business into North America. We were here largely as a result of my and Joe's combined efforts; while the guys who had come over from London were the ones who would execute that strategy at a business level alongside Joe, it was I, as Head of Strategic and Business Development, who was entrusted with driving that process.

But my sense of contentment transcended the successful initial discussions we had held in Toronto. Although I had been living in London for the past fifteen years, I had grown up less than 40 miles south of this very spot, in a small town called Dundas, Ontario. There, on the quiet suburban streets, I had played baseball with my friends late into the long summer afternoons, dreaming of one day playing for the newly established Toronto Blue Jays – the big city team that we all supported.

Well, I didn't quite make it to the Blue Jays. But 35 years later, sitting in their cavernous stadium on a beautiful spring evening, I could reflect on a job reasonably well done until this point.

Things had been going well for me in the Bank. I was earning more money than I ever had, playing a key role in the development and execution of the strategy of our business from the financial monolith known as the City of London. This North American 'summit' was a demonstration of my capacity to collaborate effectively with my senior colleagues, and to drive and co-ordinate a complex initiative. I had received very positive feedback in my recent performance review. I had the respect of my peers and the support and confidence of my boss. It was looking good - bonuses were due to be paid in less than a month and I was eagerly anticipating a further pay rise. I was back where I had been born and brought up, and felt that in some kind of cosmic way, my life had come full circle.

My musings were brought to an end by one final cheer from the crowd signalling the game's conclusion. As we shuffled out of the stadium, the home fans raucous in their victory celebrations, I was grateful that the five star hotel we were staying in was so nearby. After a long day of meetings, plus a ball game and a few beers, I was tired. We needed to be up early for a 6;30 am flight to New York and the next stage of our meetings. Exciting times and lots of change lay ahead as we developed things on this side of the pond; they would require my full energy and attention. But after a few twists and turns in the road, at the age of 42, I was up for it. I was proud of what I had achieved and optimistic about my future. I felt as if I was in my prime. I had arrived.

Until the world proved to be more fickle than I ever could have imagined...

May 12th

My legs were working like pistons but I didn't feel like I was getting anywhere. I could feel my heart beating hard within my chest. I was struggling for breath as if the air was being sucked out of my lungs. The trickle of sweat down my back had become a waterfall. I couldn't think of anything but the pain. My vision narrowed. I closed my eyes and clenched my fists, willing this to be over. My mind began to shut down. I felt confused and angry and alone. I was a well educated, intelligent, adult man. What had I done to deserve this fate? How had it come to this? Why was this happening to me? How had I allowed this to happen? How would it all end?

With my last ounce of will power, I forced my eyes opened and focussed ahead.

A surge of conflicting emotions pulsed through me, but amidst the acute suffering and sense of inadequacy, I couldn't help but feel the unbridled joy of spending a crisp spring Sunday morning running through Hampstead Heath with the one woman alive whom I didn't mind being faster than me. For only a few paces in front, facing me with that coy, half-mocking, fully loving smile was the lean figure of Tanya, all decked out in her running kit. Grime and sweat streaked her face. Yet, as always, there was the innate sense of modesty that seemed to permanently accompany Tanya, whether running up an incline in the Heath, draped in a hospital gown during labour at the nearby Royal Free, or speaking to a conference hall packed with 400 people about psychological well-being (her day job when she isn't taking care of the boys or emasculating me on long distance runs). There is an almost unearthly sense of inner grace and self-effacing charm that Tanya exudes, and with nothing to do but try and breathe as my gaze settled upon her, I could luxuriate in thinking of her sublime qualities – and how fortunate I was to bear witness to them daily.

But waxing lyrical about my wife wasn't going to get me through this ordeal; one last immense effort was still required. With a super-human final push, I caught up with Tanya and made it to the crest of the hill. Doubled over, my chest heaving, I drew breath with manic intensity. As my senses and sanity slowly returned, I cursed inwardly, chastising myself for the umpteenth time that morning for not heading to the gym while the love of my life loped amongst the squirrels and the bounding Labradors under the wizened oak branches of the glorious Heath.

I guess that's where I made my first mistake; I mean after all these years, I really should have known better. Tanya didn't run – she raced. Friends (only close ones) likened her physique to a gazelle's. And that's before they'd seen her in her Asics trainers and Nike running gloves (we have always been multi brand people). She was the perfect synthesis of sleek elegance, powerful grace and incomparable - at least in relation to me - stamina. Add to that a mind that didn't really understand pain the way most normal people do - I mean how can you be expected to compete with six natural childbirths? - and you're left with a lean, mean, running machine.

So when Tanya suggested we go for a "little run in the Heath", I should have come up with something better than; "Uh, I thought I'd do a bit of an abs workout at the gym this morning instead." Then again, I only have myself to blame for creating this running monster in the first place. For it was I who encouraged her to join Virgin Active after Rafi, our fifth son, was born ten years ago. And it was definitely I who advised her to just get on the treadmill and give it a try. And you guessed it; it was I who insisted that she try running outdoors, something she had never even contemplated before. And it was I, that genius in recognising undiscovered athletic potential, who bundled her into the car one crisp spring Sunday morning, drove us down to Regents Park, pointed smugly at the path and blithely uttered the words that I would forever regret; "Come on, let's run!"

On reflection, maybe I'm being a bit hard on myself. Being Jewish, you'd probably have to go back to the

Chariots of Fire days to remember the last time my religion produced a great athlete. When we were dating, Tanya had never expressed the slightest interest or aptitude for running. For the first ten years of our marriage, her idea of exercise was to sweep the floor vigorously after dinner. I on the other hand, by the time of that infamous Regents Park excursion, was already the veteran of four London Marathons and countless other races. I was runner up for Victor Ludorum – that's best all around athlete, not leading Latin student - in my final year of high school. Okay, fair enough, at five foot, six inches in my trainers, I wasn't exactly going to be mistaken for Usain Bolt's younger brother. Nonetheless, I was meant to be the runner in the family, not her!

Clearly, I needed to get over myself.

As my breathing slowly receded from a level resembling a heart patient in cardiac arrest, I silently instructed myself to banish these unhelpful thoughts from my mind. True, she had almost killed me on that final climb and made me wonder momentarily if this was the most devious scheme ever devised for claiming a spouse's life insurance money. But as I've already explained, this was the mother of my six children, my wife of nineteen years and the person who would be cooking me dinner tonight - assuming I didn't say anything really vengeful on the descent like; your running style resembles a sleep deprived pregnant elephant on steroids.

"Get it together," I told myself. "She's faster, fitter and thinner than you. Let it go and move on!"

This intense moment of self-reflection over, I forced myself upright and shuffled over to where she stood serenely. My eyes followed hers and together we looked down at the panoramic view of the nation's capital from the top of Parliament Hill. The early morning mist was clearing and we could see for miles; much of the city laid spread out below us. Squinting slightly, I could make out some of London's most famous landmarks; the brand new, gleaming Shard, the City's tallest structure; the colossal London Eye on the South Bank of the Thames; the famous 'Gherkin' building on the eastern edge of the Square Mile; the cluster of towering buildings that constituted the capitalist phenomenon known as Canary Wharf. And tucked away somewhere just out of view, as famous and significant as any of them; St. Paul's Cathedral.

You may be wondering why a Jewish guy from North West London regards St. Paul's as so significant. After all, I've never prayed, toured or even protested there. True, I did stand on tiptoes at the base of its hallowed front steps at the end of the glorious summer of 2012 to watch the Olympic Parade go past, catching a glimpse of Jess, Mo, Sir Chris and Wiggo's sideburns, but that's about as close as I ever got to going inside one of the world's most famous places of worship.

No, St. Paul's significance for me is a far more prosaic one. It's the tube stop I had been using every Monday to Friday for the past six years. (I had discovered that it was quicker than taking the Northern Line all the way down to Bank). Like millions of other Londoners, I seemed to spend a disturbingly disproportionate amount of my life underground, being transported to my place of employment, trying my best not to smile at anyone while surreptitiously reading somebody else's *Evening Standard* from underneath the crook of a third person's armpit. Ah, the joys of commuting.

So there we were, gazing down at the vista of one of the world's largest and most feted cities, when a thought snuck up on me. It was something that had been niggling within for a while, but in that moment, it announced itself as a major source of concern in my mind. Tanya was already turning back to the path and re-inserting the earphones of her iPod, so I knew I had to act fast. I needed to say something - any articulation of this thought, however embryonic, would do – as the slightest semblance of a meaningful discussion was my only hope of being saved from the unstinting physical and psychological torture this woman was putting me through.

"Something's up with Tony!" I blurted out.

For a moment, I thought I'd left it too late. Searching for her Marathon Playlist as she fiddled with the mini device which had forever changed the course of music history, I was sure I was done for. Any second now and Tanya would be bounding up towards Kenwood House listening to the Killers' classic *Are You Human?* while I'd be desperately searching my memory for the name of that divorce lawyer who had taken care of Donna and Stan's situation a couple of years back.

But then she turned around, her soft gentle eyes fixed on me and the voice as tender as the day we met. "What do you mean?" she asked quietly.

"I'm not too sure, but I just know something's up with him. He hasn't been the same the last few weeks and I'm a bit concerned."

Tanya looked thoughtfully at me for a moment. Then, taking my hand, we began moving forwards together, finding our special rhythm, as always.

"Tell me about it," she said. So I did.

Tony Gemgato - my boss. Tall, slightly chunky and with a mane of black hair just beginning to grey at the edges,

Tony possessed the natural authority of someone who was good at what he did. For 25 years, he had worked hard and made money – lots of it – in the City of London. Now, at the height of his powers, as the UK Head of Investment and Commercial Banking – or ICB as it was known - for SKBK Bank, Tony was responsible for 30% of the firm's global profits. He was King of the first floor, the hub of the firm's origination, syndication, distribution, securitisation and trading activities. (The casual reader may be unfamiliar with some of these modern day banking terminologies; for further edification, please refer to *The Idiot's Guide to Inexplicable Financial Engineering*, an outstanding description of contemporary banking activities co-written by three former Financial Services CEOs currently serving between five and eight years in prison.) In the four years that he had held this position, ICB had been core to the profitable financial performance of the Bank. Tony's strategy was reasonably clear; churn the balance sheet, constantly reinvesting profits without increasing capital outlay, skimming fees and margins along the way. Some people within the Bank called it 'Gemgatonomics' and saw him as a kind of financial hero. Others viewed it as irresponsible banking and called him 'risky'.

The truth, as it so often does, probably lay somewhere in between. There was no question that Tony was an aggressive banker, constantly devising new ways of maximising returns and creatively accounting for them. He pushed hard, keeping us constantly focussed on the holy grail of increasing P & L year on year. (P & L stands for Profit and Loss, which is a key metric for any business.) He set big targets and highly ambitious budgets; we never achieved them, but we thought big and dreamed bigger.

For a small, growing, foreign bank like ours trying to get a foothold in the most competitive financial market this side of the Atlantic, that kind of aspiration was important. It drove us forward, making us feel that perhaps this small fish in this very big pond could one day become a big fish that owned a fair chunk of that pond.

You're probably thinking that Tony sounds like the quintessential, stereotypical modern day banker; Michael Douglas' Gordon Gekko with a British accent and glasses. Or any one of half a dozen senior bankers who have made the front pages of the newspaper over the last few years, inevitably for the wrong reasons, since the onset of the Global Financial Crisis that changed the landscape of the world's economy. But nothing could be further from the truth. Tony was soft spoken, introverted almost. He abhorred confrontation and engaging with large groups. One to one he was affable and relaxed; a pleasure to talk with. Mention how his beloved West Bromwich Albion performed on Saturday and the conversation could go on for hours. (Admittedly that's a bit of an exaggeration; there's only so much even the most ardent fan can say about the Baggies.) But put him in a room full of people and he retreated into himself, almost like the kid on the playground who doesn't feel that he's allowed to join the footie game. Communication was his Achilles heel. Everyone knew he was immensely focussed and super clever, but it was hard to figure out what was going on inside his head. He thought inwardly, relying on others to intuit his thinking. If you didn't ask, he didn't tell. And if you did ask, he only told you some of it, always keeping his cards close to his chest. The rest you had to try and figure out for yourself.

And that was where I fitted in. Having worked closely with Tony for a few years in my consulting capacity as part of the Organisational Effectiveness team, I knew where the gaps lay in his management style and the divisional structure. So mustering up the courage one cold winter morning just after New Year's Day, 2012, I asked Tony if he could spare some time for a quick chat. He readily agreed in his affable way and a few minutes later we were sitting at the long table in Room 105. As was almost always the case with us, the conversation opened with a quick round-up of our team's respective performances. There had just been the usual frenetic programme of matches over the Christmas period, so there was a lot to discuss.

"Do you think you guys can keep City at bay?" Tony enquired. "They're looking really strong, especially the way Silva and Aguero are playing at the moment."

"I don't know," I replied somewhat evasively. "They definitely have the stronger squad, but then again, we've got the best manager. That will count for a lot of points come the end of season. How about you guys? Do you think your manager has taken them as far as they can go?"

"That's hard to tell," responded Tony, trying to sound as neutral as possible. "I think he's very under-rated. It's true we're not that pretty to watch but he always keeps us up."

And so we carried on for a while, the pressures of the City briefly ignored as we both indulged our true passion. Eventually though, I had to take the plunge.

"Uh, Tony, I wanted to ask you whether you'd ever be interested in a guy like me joining the division proper and playing a more hands-on role in the development of the business."

Smoothly accepting the changing of gears, Tony got straight to the point. "Are you thinking strategy or client facing?" he asked.

"Strategy."

"Yes, I would be. I think you've got the skills to help us a lot and I've been looking to build a strategy and development team anyhow. Sounds good. Let me chew it over and discuss it with a couple of the senior guys and I'll get back to you soon."

A couple of months later, Tony officially 'poached' me from the OE team where I had been since joining the firm. Though I knew it might ruffle some feathers with the guys I was leaving behind, not to mention my previous boss, I jumped at the opportunity to join the business side and report directly to Tony when he offered me the role. Who wouldn't? It was a great chance to work in a senior position at the heart of the most successful division in the firm. And it gave me the opportunity to shift away from consulting, continuing my career advancement from the epicentre of the business.

Relocating to sit directly next to Tony in the middle of our large, open-plan trading floor, my new role was a unique creation of Tony's - and a direct result of the peculiarities of his personal style of leadership. Tony wasn't great on engaging; I thrived on it. Tony was pretty hands-off with most things; I was more of an 'in your face' kind of guy. Tony saw communication as a necessary evil; I saw it as what I did best. Tony found committees, forums and large meetings a waste of time; I couldn't get enough of them (well, not quite, but you get the idea). I was the guy who could communicate on his behalf to the rest of the division and engage people and specific projects in a visible and energised way. Or at least that's what I put down on the self-assessment section of my performance review.

Somebody on the floor once referred to me as "Tony's brain". I took that as a big, if highly inaccurate compliment. Tony's brain worked just fine and didn't need any intervention from mine. But what I think he meant was that he saw me as the guy who understood Tony's mind, had a finger on the pulse of his thinking, and most importantly, could share those thoughts with others on the floor. Officially, my job description was to implement the Executive's strategic plans to develop and expand our business, both geographically and in terms of new business lines. Unofficially, I was Tony's go-to man for all things not involving derivatives, hedging, collateralised loan obligations and any of those other exotic things that made lots of money. It was a good gig that paid well enough, and perhaps more importantly to me, meant that I was a key lieutenant to one of the Bank's most successful and influential business leaders.

But ever since I had returned from the latest round of North American meetings a couple of weeks ago, Tony had seemed different somehow. His rhythm had become erratic; his focus ever so slightly distracted. He was arriving at the office increasingly late, leaving that discernible drop early, and was frustratingly reluctant to commit to certain key initiatives we had been working on for months. These changes may not have been obvious to many, but to those of us who knew him well and worked closely with him, we could sense something was going on. For a man renowned for his singularly one-dimensional pursuit of profit, the subtle changes in his focus couldn't be ignored. Yet the problem lay in interpreting what they meant. Little did I know that I wouldn't need to wait long to get an answer.

May 15th

The diary invitation had merely said 'Special Exco Meeting.' But we all knew that some major news was about to break. A 9 am meeting called the night before was extraordinary, especially considering Tony's well-known aversion to meetings and communications. This was going to be big. It was exactly 72 hours since Tanya had tried to kill me while running in the Heath and I had an uneasy feeling that my "something is up with Tony" comment was about to receive some serious elaboration.

As we settled down at the long rectangular table in Room 105, I looked around at my colleagues on the ICB Executive Committee. Each of them ran one of the ten businesses which made up the Investment and Commercial Banking division. Between them, I estimated somewhat smugly, there was as much experience of financial services as you would find in any room of similar size in the City. This was a highly motivated, exceptionally talented team of people. These guys were hungry and ambitious. They knew how to take money and make more money out of it. We may not have been the biggest or noisiest boys on the block – think Swansea City, not Manchester City – but man for man (with the exception of Maxine, who was a woman) I wouldn't have swapped them for anyone.

Aside from their obvious financial nous, they were by and large, thoroughly decent people. Sure, each of us had our own idiosyncrasies – Ray for example moonlighted as a drummer in the aptly named rock band Wall Street – but we shared a common vision and every seat at that table was filled by a highly intelligent, capable person whose business unit contributed towards the achievement of that vision. The only exceptions, in the sense that neither of us was specifically responsible for running a revenue generating team, were Maxine, the divisional Head of Finance, and me.

The sense that something dramatic was about to happen was heightened when Tony walked past his normal seat at the head of the table, instead positioning himself in the chair just to its left. Moments later, the significance of that arrangement was confirmed when Rupert unexpectedly walked through the door and seated his large, six foot, three inch frame in that seat instead. Rupert Evans was our CEO, the head of the entire UK Bank. Like Tony, he defied the stereotypical perception of a senior City banker. Though my personal work interactions with Rupert over the years had been limited to occasional meetings regarding specific initiatives I was working on, I had come to respect and appreciate his calm demeanour, slight shyness and thoughtful approach. His languid, almost laconic manner belied a fierce intellect and intense ambition. People experienced Rupert as grounded and down-to-earth, reflected by his penchant for taking the overland train to work. We would often bump into each other in the side entrance lift at the conclusion of our respective commutes, his backpack strung over his shoulder and his national train card poking out of his back pocket, a look entirely in keeping with his slightly unkempt appearance. Those who were new to the bank would never have known they were sharing the lift with the Big Boss.

Well, the Big Boss was in the house now and things were about to change.

"Thanks for coming at short notice guys," Rupert began, crossing his long legs and looking across the table. He turned ever so slightly towards Tony before continuing.

"So we wanted to let you all know that Tony has decided to retire after 25 years in the City. He'll be leaving pretty quickly and we wanted you to hear the news first before the official announcement goes out. I just wanted to thank Tony for everything he's done for us over the past few years. He's left the division in a far stronger position than when he joined, and I'm sure you'll all join me in wishing Tony the best of luck and much enjoyment in spending more time with his family. Of course it goes without saying that everyone should just continue with business as usual for the moment. Uh, Tony, is there anything you'd like to say?"

Tony, ever the great communicator, briefly thanked everyone for their contributions over the time he'd been running things, and somewhat incongruously finished off with; "You've all been good friends and it's been a lot of fun. Thanks."

So that was it. Bombshell dropped. Something had been up with Tony. The erratic schedule, the lack of focus, the ambivalence to commit – it all made sense suddenly. What I had said to Tanya on the Heath only three days earlier had indeed been a portent and now we all knew what it was; Tony was gone and things were going to change. As Rupert got up from his chair, signalling to the rest of us that this briefest of meetings was over, it was just beginning to dawn on me that my own little world was starting to shift on its axis; I had no idea yet how great that shift would be. And as we began shuffling out of the room, vacating the remaining chairs, I wondered which seat I would be sitting in, if any, when the music stopped.

May 22nd

A lot had happened over the past seven days. True to his introverted personality, Tony had left the business to very little fanfare that same day - no long drawn out goodbyes or dramatic messages to the multitudes. I was sorry to see Tony go. Not just because he had been my sponsor and supporter in the business who had given me my opportunity, nor even because we shared a love for football that is so hard to find with another man these days (you know what I mean). Tony had been a good boss. He had identified my strengths and played to them; he knew my weaknesses and gaps and avoided them dextrously. And he was a genuinely nice guy; relaxed, easy-going, treated you as an equal.

I - and he - wanted to say goodbye to each other properly. So that same morning, shortly after the meeting with Rupert, we met for the last chat we would ever have in Room 105. Tony began by apologising for not being able to let me know his news earlier.

"Sorry if this came as a big surprise Brian. But the Regulator insisted we had to keep things quiet until we were ready to make an official announcement."

I didn't quite get it, but let it go, instead trying to get a better understanding of what was behind his decision to leave.

"I've been doing this for a long time - over 25 years," Tony explained when I asked him why he had arrived at this conclusion now. "I've done okay, made the kind of money I wanted to make," he continued. (Talk about understatement!) "I'd been thinking about this for a few months already. And I just felt it was time to go, to spend more time with my kids, to put an end to all this commuting. I've really enjoyed it and am proud of what we've achieved, but I'm about to turn 50 – it's enough now."

Though compelling, it didn't completely stack up for me, so I tried to press him. I know we had missed our targets at the most recent round of budget reviews; perhaps there was something more sinister at play.

"Did you feel any pressure from above?" I asked brazenly.

Ever the diplomat, Tony reassured me that the decision was entirely his. "No, it was just the right time."

I'm not entirely sure if I believed him. In the end though, it didn't matter. Tony had left, and in his wake, the casualties were beginning to mount.

Tony's sudden resignation set off a chain reaction. First went Dick Bear, Tony's closest ally in the business and the individual responsible for all those securitisations, syndications and collateralised loan obligations that had seemed to confuse not just me, but seemingly most other people in the Bank as well. Some of Dick's key guys also looked to be heading out the door; his entire team was being dismantled and re-integrated into other desks in the business. Meanwhile, some of the key projects I had been working on – North American expansion, the Channel Islands, a restructured Credit Committee – had been put on hold indefinitely. We seemed to be in a period of suspended animation and people were overtly tense on the floor, myself included. Nobody knew who or what was next.

Craig Hertford, a friend and erstwhile protégé of Rupert's, had been appointed to take over and was already talking about doing things differently. He had looked under the bonnet, so to speak, and it was obvious that changes were afoot. A couple of senior colleagues had told me that Craig had asked them for their views and help in getting to grips with the strategy and activities of some of the key business desks. Significantly, Craig had not asked that of me, which didn't bode well. The inner circle was reforming and it looked like I wasn't part of it any longer; I was starting to feel increasingly like I was on the outside looking in.

Feeling unusually insecure, I cornered Erik, a co-member of the Exco, by the Nespresso machine a couple of days after Craig's appointment. "What do you think of everything that's going down?" I asked him as casually as I could. "I haven't spoken to Craig since he took over – do you reckon he's going to keep the Strategy role as it is?"

Erik was one of the smartest guys in the business and undoubtedly one of our biggest revenue producers. He was Scandinavian with a typically fair complexion, full of blonde hair, crude jokes and politically incorrect utterances. A fellow member of the Executive Committee, I had come to see first-hand how his brain understood complex trading transactions quicker than just about anybody in the division. He was one of the Bank's genuine rainmakers and his team's sheer contribution to profitability made him one of the safest guys on the floor amidst all the upheaval. We got along well – I liked his directness and caustic sense of humour and will always be grateful to him for introducing me to Hendricks Gin (Thursday evening date nights with Tanya have never been the same since).

Placing a hand on my shoulder and looking me straight in the eye while his coffee frothed noisily behind us, Erik bolstered me with characteristic bluntness; "You're an SKBK guy. And everyone around here likes you. Don't worry, you'll be fine."

Although Erik was better known for making a profit than dispensing prophecy, I was comforted by his reassurance. Still, the continued absence of any contact with Craig worried me. Try as I did, I couldn't avoid the gnawing sense of something not being quite right.

I knew Craig well and had worked with him quite closely in the OE role before joining the division proper. In my opinion, and that of many others in the business, he was one of the best up and coming leaders we had. He was smart, polished and intensely focussed. He had spent the last five years building up a whole new business line called Corporate Transactions and Treasury. He hadn't blown the lights out, but that was not Craig's style. He was methodical and consistent, committed to building an annuity-type business that showed year-on-year growth and which was relatively immune to market fluctuation. At six feet, two inches, with a full crop of dark hair and a rugby player's physique, Craig was an impressive guy. Aged 43, he was in his intellectual and physical prime. He'd just got the big promotion and the career of Craig Hertford was clearly on a major upward trajectory.

Prior to taking the Strategy role under Tony, I had helped Craig with a number of issues as part of my consulting responsibility to his business. I had advised him on a few major staff decisions and individual performance issues. I had co-designed and facilitated a couple of team-building sessions and strategic conferences for his desk. We'd always got along well and had mutual respect for each other. As a matter of fact, when I was back in the OE team, he had been one of my key internal 'clients' and supporters. I counted Craig as a friend and the right choice to lead the business forward in the wake of Tony's departure.

But all of that was irrelevant now. Business was business and Craig was the new boss. My fate, as dramatic as that sounds, was in his hands.

So when I received an invitation in my Outlook Calendar to meet Craig in Room 105 exactly a week after he had taken over, I felt a strange mix of anxiety and relief. On the one hand, I was apprehensive, uncertain what to expect. Craig's obvious avoidance of me since his appointment created a nagging worry in the back of my mind. On the other hand, the meeting was an opportunity to finally establish where things were going from here, and more importantly, what that meant for me.

I prepared thoroughly for the meeting. Earlier that morning, I booked out a couple of hours in my diary and had taken myself off to the Starbucks in Paternoster Square to think, plan and make some notes. Aware that key strategic and expansion projects were under review, I wanted to be able to demonstrate to Craig the different initiatives I had been working on and the progress I thought we were making. I also wanted to throw a few new ideas at him regarding how we could shape the strategy of the division and develop further revenue opportunities in new business lines and jurisdictions. A couple of skinny cappuccinos later, I felt ready for my first encounter with Craig since he had been made Head. I wasn't sure what he had in his mind or where he saw things going, but at least I felt I had done my part - if he asked.

Taking the lift to the first floor, I made a quick right past the guest facilities (that's a euphemism for the loo), then a left, arriving at Room 105 directly in front of me. Pausing for a moment to compose myself and adjust my tie, I looked through the glass window of the doorframe. Craig was there already, standing by the beverage tray, spooning sugar into his coffee cup. Straightening my back ever so slightly and reminding myself one last time that I was a highly regarded, experienced employee of the Bank – an 'SKBK guy' as Erik had put it - who had much to offer the man standing on the other side of the door, I deftly turned the handle and stepped confidently into the room.

"Can I pour you a coffee?" Craig asked as I walked in...

4 Ego as vice

The only real nobility is in being superior to your former self.
Whitney Young, civil rights leader

May 23rd"
Listen Mom," I said, "you need to understand that this job wasn't necessarily that good for me. I feel like I've lost my way somehow and gone off course from the values and way of being that matter to us."

My mother looked at me as if I just told her Tanya was pregnant with quintuplets.

"I don't get what you're saying at all Brian," she said, her eyes darting to my step-father Dan for support. "You loved this job; you're good at it; they really think highly of you. And they just gave you a raise, didn't they? What you're saying doesn't make sense to me."

I looked at my mother and my heart dropped. I could see the worry etched on her slightly lined face and in her alert, olive-green eyes. It was the evening after the initial meeting with Craig and Lauren and I had come to share my news with her and my step-father. I knew she would take it hard, but this was proving to be really painful. The good thing though is that I understood why. My mother, like millions of other great mothers around the world, just wanted things to be fine, to make sense, to fit together as neatly as possible. And what I was telling her didn't really stack up. It's true – I had enjoyed my work; I was pretty good at what I did; I was well regarded and liked. And importantly for a mother, I made an honest, decent living out of it. Telling her that I was being made redundant was hard enough to understand. But suggesting that maybe it wasn't such a bad thing – that leaving the City might help me re-find my soft, squishy, more spiritual centre – was going too far. I might as well have been speaking in Swahili to her.

So let me offer some background at this point, beginning with one of my most visceral memories.

I am nine years old. We are sitting at the kitchen table, the late afternoon sun casting a light glow over the room. My father is speaking to me, gently and soothingly, but I am crying hard and can't seem to stop.

"I know this is difficult my Boy, but this is the right move for you. You'll make new friends, and still be able to see the old ones. This new school will be stimulating; they've established it especially for children like you. You'll learn how to use your mind much better than you have until now. A child of your potential should be in an environment and amongst classmates that will truly help you to thrive."

My parents were not the pushy types, at least not explicitly so. But an opportunity had arisen which they felt could not be ignored. The recent IQ testing at my local primary school which I had been attending – the aptly named Pleasant Valley Primary School - had shown up some unusually high marks. Now, just in case you're thinking I was some kind of child genius/prodigy, it's worth noting that intelligence testing was, as it still is today, an imperfect science. My 'gifted scores' were only in certain areas – nobody was predicting a future for me as a nuclear physicist or a mathematician. But there was enough evidence in the language and creative parts of the test that suggested I would benefit from being educated at a new school that had just been established in a nearby town. I was desperate not to leave Pleasant Valley for Fessenden Primary (I mean just listen to those names, can you blame me?) to join the newly created programme for those of us who apparently required extra stimulation and imaginative teaching methods. But as I said, based on the advice given by the educational 'experts' at the time, my parents felt they had little choice. So off I went to join the 'clever kids.'

Many years later, my mother confided in me that she regretted this decision. Before, I had been a happy, well adjusted, regular kid hanging out with children of the same ilk; but the change of school didn't work out for me. Not only did I never win a Nobel Prize, I never really settled in the new school. I struggled somewhat in the new environment, socially and emotionally. They had told me my intelligence was a big asset; that's what I was doing there. But I felt lonely and out of place. I didn't want to be special; I just wanted to be me.

My mother, to her credit, had belatedly come to realise this. But I don't think even she recognised the effect this change of school had on me. For the die had been cast, the script written. It left an indelible imprint on my self-image. I had been told I was very clever; it's what made me different. Despite my initial resistance, what choice did I have but to believe them?

And so, an adult-size ego was born to a nine-year old kid who did pretty well on a primitive IQ test. Now ego, in my opinion, is one of the most misunderstood terms out there. For starters, most people assume it has a pejorative connotation; ego involuntarily becomes associated with words like arrogance, narcissism, vanity, selfishness, self-importance and conceit (I'm sure there are others but that's all my thesaurus on Microsoft Word came up with.) Alternatively, for those of us with a psychodynamic bent, we tend to think of ego in terms of Id, super-ego and other Freudian concepts. Ego has become a big part of the modern lexicon, though psychoanalysts tend to throw this term around a little too liberally for my liking, charging £80 a week over a 17 year period for the privilege.

But I am not thinking of ego as a good or a bad thing – it is not so binary in nature. We all have an ego – without it we'd likely be saints, prophets or clones of Angelina Jolie. The question is not whether or not you have an ego. The question is how dominant is it? Is it more or less under control most of the time, or is it ruling you? Is it framing the way you think; the key decisions you make; your way of showing up in the world? Still, in my case my ego probably would have found its equilibrium over time had it not been for the establishment of a formidable partnership. It needed a faithful ally – and found one in my unbridled ambition.

Most men can probably recall the last time they cried in their mother's arms. Mine took place when I was sixteen years old (admittedly a bit late, but then again, I *was* a late bloomer.) The First Team Rugby XV had just been announced – and I wasn't in it. As the incumbent in the position for the past three seasons in secondary school, I was considered favourite to be named as the starting scrum-half. While I was small and slight, I was also quick, wispy and technically competent. I had trained throughout the autumn on the bone-hard South African school pitches, passing and kicking over and over until I achieved unerring accuracy. I couldn't do much about my size (I've bulked up since, having ruled out steroids at the time) but my fitness and form were as good as could be; a starting berth in the most important team in the most important sport at my school had been there for the taking.

One problem; the new coach, the ridiculously named Rassie Erasmus, decided this was the moment he wanted to go modern; he was seeking a scrum-half who was bigger, stronger and more powerful. My luck was out - Coach Rassie's vision was about fifteen years before its time. Step forward David, one of my best mates, whose entire rugby career until now had been spent as a hooker in the front row. Not anymore; David fitted the prototype of what the new coach was looking for, and suddenly my place in the side had come under serious threat. The fact that he could pass farther and run faster than me probably didn't help my chances either. Nothing was more important to a sixteen year old boy than to wear the blue and white horizontal stripes of my school's first team rugby colours, but though I had a jersey, it was doomed to remain unused while I sat on the substitute's bench.

As I lay crying pitifully in my mother's embracing arms, I had to confront the shattering of the illusion to which I had been desperately clinging. Mom tried her best to alleviate my suffering, but there was little to be done. I had created a perception of myself that I had failed to live up to, and the sense of crushing disappointment which accompanied that failure was simply too much to bear. I had constructed a self-image predicated on being a First Team rugby player. When that failed to materialise, when my perception of myself was exposed as overly ambitious, I was crestfallen. I was only sixteen, but already I had developed a seriously grandiose ambition; over-reaching, unrealised and unfulfilled, I had become trapped in its vice.

Over the next few years, as I transitioned from teenager to border-line adult, my ego continued relatively unencumbered on its own trajectory. That seemingly unstoppable process was finally impeded by a speed-bump that appeared in the form of some quite unexpected encounters in the ancient, holy city of Jerusalem when I was nineteen.

It had never been part of my plans to explore a more spiritual, meaningful life. I was brought up in a secular home. We were Jewish in a cultural sense, so some of the key traditions like the Passover Seder and lighting candles on a Friday night were observed, but that was pretty much the extent of religion in our lives. It was a casual relationship to faith, devoid of significant meaning and commitment. Our home was always full of books, ideas and interesting dialogue covering politics, literature, history, the arts and professional wrestling (though admittedly the final topic was more of a monologue which I had with myself.) My parents were both intellectual moralists who took life and their responsibilities in the world seriously. But growing up in my home, I never recalled hearing the term *spirituality*, and I certainly never experienced any relationship to the spiritual world.

That changed for me during my gap year. Fresh out of high school, my southern hemisphere winter of 1990 had been spent in the glorious heat and sunshine of a Mediterranean summer. It started with realising a once in a lifetime dream to attend *Italia 90* - the World Cup Finals in Italy (as a spectator mind you, not a player in case you were wondering.) Having experienced heaven already at the ripe old age of nineteen, I flew to Israel the day after the final in Rome's Olympic Stadium to join up with some old school friends who were halfway through a year's programme at Jerusalem's Hebrew University. But I quickly became bored; while they were attending classes in the day, I found myself strolling aimlessly around the Mount Scopus campus looking for something to do. (Trying to decide whether to have humus or tachina on my pita in the cafeteria didn't quite compare with the excitement I had experienced a week earlier of being in the stadium as Maradonna rolled a penalty down the middle of the goal to knock the hosts out of the World Cup and send Argentina into a final with West Germany.) So when I stumbled upon some lads I vaguely knew who recommended I attend a lecture at a Jewish learning academy that specialised in programmes for beginners – images of Barbara Streissand's *Yentl* began appearing unhelpfully in my mind – I agreed to give it a shot. One lecture led to another, and then another, until I decided to extend my initial two week trip and find out a bit more about this Judaism and spirituality thing.

I quickly became exposed to a completely different world, where people spoke constantly about God, faith and the spiritual world. Some of them seemed enlightened to me, their faces radiating an almost unearthly glow of deep connectivity and inner harmony. I met and studied with some truly extraordinary people – scholars immersed in sacred texts whose souls seemed to touch worlds beyond any I could envisage, and who's almost saintly personal conduct far exceeded anything I had previously experienced. For me, a relatively privileged, somewhat superficial young man on the cusp of the grown-up world of adults, these holy people and their lifestyle represented a whole new universe – and it was a universe that for all its lack of familiarity, held a compelling attraction for me.

I soon returned to South Africa (my three month ticket was about to expire) and over the next few years, I gradually became absorbed in the world of Jewish thought, ethics, study and practice. This led to some external changes in my appearance and a reconfiguring of some of my culinary preferences and use of language (four letter words were out; so was my earring, long hair and fondness for non-kosher cheeseburgers.) It's true that I was changing, but to most observers, it was for the better.

The narcissistic, passive-aggressive guy with a predisposition towards self-indulgence was gradually replaced by a more moral, genuine, caring and softer version. Some may say this is just the normal process of maturing, and they may be right. But something else was at play here and it started to seep in. Being a good person, working on my rough edges and aspiring for an experience that transcended the self had begun to take root. Looking beyond my own needs and considering how I could contribute into the world and develop meaningful relationships began to matter. My soul had been touched, and as I began to explore what that meant, it became obvious to me and my poor parents - who now had to dine with me at over-priced kosher restaurants and listen to my frequently self-righteous sermonising - that there was no turning back. Enlightened I wasn't. But the game had changed and things were looking up.

Returning to the events of May 2013, and this whole business about losing my way and neglecting the things that really mattered to me, it should all be starting to make sense now. This is also where it gets a bit tricky to explain and deeply personal (on second thoughts, I already crossed that line when I revealed the episode about taking a family friend to the high school dance), so bear with me. It's true that Tanya, the Boys and I were committed to our religion – in some ways, we had become model members of the community. I attended synagogue daily and tried to fit in a regular study session as well. I was even persuaded once to stand for a position on our synagogue board, a decision I immediately regretted when I subsequently failed to secure enough votes to ensure my successful nomination (though I am encouraged by the little known historical fact that Abraham Lincoln failed in numerous attempts to get elected to public office before he finally hit the jackpot.) Colleagues at the bank considered me the closest thing to a religious fanatic that they had come across. Having six children and a skull-cap didn't help to dispel that notion. Fortunately, I knew more about football and indie bands than any of them, which helped to demonstrate that I did live in the real world and that being a member of the God Squad might have some upsides.

So while externally I was still the religiously committed, true to my faith guy that started that whole journey back in Israel over twenty years ago, on the inside, there had been gradual erosion. Again, I'm not talking about the obvious stuff like suddenly developing a compulsion to start stealing bacon rolls from the local kebab shop or swindling grannies and widows with complex ponzi schemes and running off to the Cayman Islands with their life savings. I'm not even talking about being taking liberties with Her Majesty's taxation requirements or finding ingenious ways to avoid paying parking fines (this is a skill that way preceded my spiritual enlightenment.) I'm talking about the kind of stuff most people don't see and wouldn't understand; those aspects that only the people who really know you – your spouse, your therapist, maybe your personal trainer if you're really lonely – know about you.

It's the stuff that starts to change within you so imperceptibly that you don't realise until it's too late. And then you wake up one day and ask yourself; is this who I wanted to become? Is this what I want to be in this world?

Those who know me reasonably well might well ask; "What's he going on about? After all, he has a wonderful wife, six healthy kids, is a well respected member of the community and supports Manchester United. He seems to be doing alright." This, of course, is true at one level. But we all know ourselves; we know when we are letting ourselves down. Just like we know what it feels like to underperform in the work environment, so too do we know the feeling that exists within us when we are underperforming in this project called our lives. And when it came to my project, I had to accept that I was not about to receive the most outstanding performance review for The Life of Brian. (With apologies to *Monty Python*.)

Now comes the tough part; identifying what that erosion was and how it was affecting both me and my family. Unsurprisingly, the waterfall of tears on the first night of redundancy was the pointer. After years of living in the background, my ego - that old chestnut - had made a Rocky-type comeback. And this time, having managed to elude the despairing clutches of my religious and spiritual aspirations, it was bigger and badder than ever before.

My ego had begun to spiral out of control. Not in an obvious way - I hadn't tried out for *Britain's Got Talent* or anything. Rather, mine was a more subtle, nuanced version of unrestrained ego. My arrogance lay not in believing I was better than others. It lay in believing my own press. My sense of self-importance had increased in direct proportion to my career success. I had convinced myself that I was well on the path – not just to a successful career, but to a successful life. I genuinely felt that I was at the top of my game; now was the time to go out and win it. (Do phrases like 'Pride before the fall' and 'I will put an end to the pomp of the arrogant' come to mind?)

In the early years of my religious journey and the subsequent years of my marriage, having kids, working in the not-for-profit sector and watching *The West Wing*, I had worked hard to subvert the ego; to attack head-on my sense of self importance and the pursuit of my own self interest at almost any cost. I hadn't always won every battle, but I felt I was pretty much winning the war ... that is, until I arrived in the City.

When I made that first commute on the Northern Line over six years ago, I was incredibly motivated about developing the next stage of my career and life. I felt giddy about the possibilities, bordering on a sense of grandiosity that I hadn't felt since I convinced myself that the only thing keeping me from being Peter Schmeichel's successor at Man U was the conviction that Sir Alex's scouting network didn't extend this far south. I was excited, optimistic and confident about the future. But I was also raw, naive and often ignorant of corporate life and banking in particular; I made clumsy errors and silly gaffes, occasionally landing myself in hot water with my boss and colleagues. I was trying to transition from ten years of working in the educational and outreach world of meaning, purpose and contribution – and it wasn't always pretty. In the infamous words of Donald Rumsfeld; "I didn't know what I didn't know."

So I set out to make sure I knew what I knew. More importantly, I set out to let others know what I knew. I made it my business to understand the Bank; how it worked; how it made money; what the risks were; and how to determine if they were worth taking. I fell back on what they had told me when I was nine years old; that I belonged with the clever kids. Believing that my greatest asset was the effective use of my intellect, I applied it rigorously to making sense of and adding value to this newly discovered world of financial services. Letting others know how much I knew became imperative; it was the only way I could close the gap in experience and expertise that existed between me and them. My brain became the most indispensible tool I had, and my gift of the gab its trusted sidekick.

All of this is not to say that I behaved ruthlessly or failed to appreciate my own temperament. I knew that I thrived under pressure, that I enjoyed being productive, that I performed better in a structured environment amongst a group of talented and ambitious colleagues, and that I was highly motivated to do well and vie with my peers. In the banking environment, without strong financial skills and experience to buttress me, I needed to strive harder and trade on my intellectual abilities, as well as my easy-going manner that gained me friends and allies in the organisation.

Over time, I established myself at the firm and gained a reputation as someone committed to upholding the organisation's values and culture. One of my most touching moments at the Bank came on a team-building weekend away; we were in the midst of giving each other feedback. This usually consisted of a platitude such as "you've got good posture and I like the new highlights in your hair" (I used to be a natural blonde so this feedback mattered to me,) which was often the entre into being eviscerated in front of the rest of the group by being told you can't spell properly, always say the wrong thing in front of clients and have terrible halitosis. But on this occasion, Candice started to say some really sweet things about how brave and kind I was, how much of an impact my integrity and honesty had on her, and how closely I resembled Ryan Gosling. (Ok, I admit; the second of those three points was not entirely true.) I was very moved by these remarks as my behaviour in the work environment and having a positive impact on my colleagues mattered a great deal to me.

But how I behaved was not my primary issue. Sure, I was considered a good corporate citizen and a decent colleague. I was reasonably well liked and the only people I ever knowingly offended in the office were the IT Helpdesk guys - and that's only because my virtual Thin Client connection kept losing connectivity. Yet that subtle slide towards egocentricity had begun and there was no turning back.

Critically - and herein lies the nub of the issue – while I did not generally *behave* self importantly, I *thought* of myself self importantly. The result is that paradoxically, while others saw me as one of the 'nice guys' who had a reputation for being helpful and supportive, I thought of myself increasingly in a different way. Winning began to matter too much, as did getting ahead. Earning more money had become a significant personal driver which it never had before. Perception and status took on a disproportionate meaning for me; vanity and self interest had found its grip and wouldn't let go. My views of myself and my future had become increasingly grandiose. In short, I had become overly attached to my own success and to myself.

While I was never going to be mistaken for being the most humble man ever to walk on this planet (that particular accolade must surely go to Simon Cowell,) I had lost my balance and begun the slide down the proverbial slippery slope. The effect was subtle and insidious, kind of like a worm eating its way from the inside out. So much of the learning generated and built upon in Jerusalem a lifetime ago was being neglected; worse, it was being corrupted. But I knew. And Tanya knew. She knew because she knew me before my career switch and corporate ladder climb – *really* knew me. And I even suspect that some of the older kids had begun to know. Or at least notice.

I had become increasingly fractious with them. My tolerance levels were at an all time low; my temper at an all time high. It would be easy to suggest that the stresses of work were the primary cause, but that would be simply untrue, or at least only part of the story. The real truth is that an ego-driven disposition and a gentle temperament are simply incompatible, for gentleness and softness only reside where humility reigns. In its absence, hardness, anger and intolerance gain traction. It's not that I had become some kind of violent, abusive monster - though I am ashamed to say that there were moments when I may not have been too far from that characterisation. But the easy-going, loving and gentle man, husband and father who once was a consistently present figure in their lives, was increasingly hard to find. On the brief occasions in which he did make a guest appearance, my kids didn't always seem to recognise him.

I wasn't ignorant of my situation – I could see the changes in me, even though I tried not to be unduly concerned by them. (In any model of psychology, this is known as denial.) I had become hard on Tanya and the kids. I would catch myself being overly critical of her and chide myself to hold back. I would be overtly judgmental of my oldest son's idiosyncrasies and then remonstrate with myself to let him be. I would engage in a destructive conflict with our most recent terrorist – I mean teenager – instead of dealing with him in a mature fashion befitting a grown man (never mind one with formal training in conflict resolution.)

There were many times when I let myself down; most seemed trivial in isolation and taken on their own, probably could be construed as such (or at least that's how I rationalised it to myself.) But taken collectively, over a period of time, the destructive effect on the family, especially the boys, couldn't be ignored.

On one such occasion, we arrived home very late one night after a relaxing evening out to discover our just-turned fourteen year old playing with the iPad on our bed, still fully clothed in his school uniform. Josh was breaking all the rules we had set him; bedtime; being alone in our bedroom; using the iPad without permission. So true to form, I hit the roof.

"What do you think you're doing?" I screamed at him, loud enough to wake the baby, which I did. "Get off of my bed, get out of my room!" I ranted.

He retreated quickly, but I wasn't done yet. Following – or more like chasing – him down to his bedroom, I forced the door open as he cowered behind it. "You've violated our trust. You're pathetic! You're grounded indefinitely!" I was out of control. "What's the matter with you?" I bellowed like some kind of sadistic maniac.

But that was the wrong question. The real question – which no one in the house dared to ask while my rage ran amok – was; what was the matter with me?

I knew I was letting myself - and the family down. I felt bad about it and wished it to change. I tried multiple approaches; prayer, self-recrimination, watching old episodes of *Friends*. But the change was never deep or lasting. I kept feeling like I had hit a roadblock that I couldn't overcome.

My ego had become too dominant, too influential. While much of the time I managed to keep it pretty well hidden, the reality was very different. I often felt like a wolf in lamb's clothing, but unlike in the children's nursery rhyme, the little ones could see clearly through the act; my big teeth were too obvious and too incongruent to keep up the charade much longer. I *needed* the illusion to be exposed, for their sake, for my sake, for all our sakes.

The nature of all illusions is that that they are transient. The wave I was on was going to crash; the only question was how much I'd be hurting when I resurfaced. My salvation, though I didn't know it yet, lay in getting my ego – my unrestrained self - out of the way. And I just needed something or someone to be the catalyst, because I was finding myself incredibly difficult to dislodge on my own.

So along comes a whole series of events not entirely of my own making, to provide me with exactly that opportunity. It was beginning to dawn on me that if I desired it enough – if I really *chose* it to be so – my redundancy could be the best thing that ever happened to me. It could be the sword that I could wield to slay that rampant ego, once and for all. Even though it was only twenty-four hours since I had been made redundant, I was already feeling very different inside. However disconcerting it felt, something about that inner shift had an increasingly cathartic quality to it.

Which brings me back to Mom. Perhaps her greatest personal quality is her capacity to listen, to absorb, to process and to slowly arrive at a different understanding of things. And of course she understood my situation and inner thoughts better than just about anyone. She knows me pretty well; after all, she is my Mom.

As we talked it through, she began to understand what I was saying; that my time at the Bank had accentuated the parts of me that I wasn't too proud of; that there was a side of me that had been subverted in my quest to 'make it' out there. Being my mother, she wasn't about to commit to a full frontal assault on my ego – she'd leave that to my loving wife. But she began to see that I aspired to live, think and act in a way that felt more congruent with my core values and authentic self.

Still Mom worried about us and our future; she didn't agree with everything I was saying nor did it all make complete sense to her. Actually, we may never see eye to eye on all of this. But that doesn't matter, and it's not the ultimate goal. More important is that Mom, and others who play significant roles in our lives, will have a better idea of what I am going on about as I try to make sense of this all.

This is particularly important in Mom's case, for were she not able to arrive at some kind of acceptance of what I was saying, I fear we might soon be visiting her in the asylum, where she'd be babbling incoherently in Swahili to her therapist about soft, squishy centres, egos laid waste by redundant swords and the inexplicable, instantaneous addition of five more grandchildren.

5. Difficulties in letting go

The world we have created is a product of our way of thinking
Albert Einstein

May 24th
It was two days after being informed I was being made redundant. I had put off making the phone call as long as I could. There is a fine line between procrastination and cowardice; if I didn't call my father-in-law Barry soon, I was going to cross that line.

If you think I'm being a bit melodramatic, consider the following for a moment; you go on a date with a successful businessman's eldest daughter, who one month previously still had 'teen' affixed to her age description. Five weeks later, without going through that old-fashioned 'asking permission thing', you propose. You have an undergraduate degree in the Arts, which is not exactly synonymous with consistent annuity earning potential. When you mention that you majored in Feminist Literature, he responds by asking what kind of competitive advantage that gives you. You casually mention that you are considering training to become a rabbi and he responds by asking how much that costs. You articulate your long-term domestic strategy of immigrating to Israel and living off an eclectic mix of government benefits, educational stipends and your late grandmother's small inheritance, and he rolls his eyes.

Over the following few years, I managed to become reasonably well respected in the community, a half decent father, a pretty good husband and a (very) minor celebrity in the local Jewish press for being one half of the only husband-and-wife team around to have run the London Marathon together. I was also broke and mortgaged to the hilt – and no prize for guessing who had put up most of the down payment on the house in the first place.

By now, you should be getting the picture. I may have been a nice guy who was committed to loving, honouring and obeying this man's daughter – but when it came to living in the world of adults, I didn't have a clue.

So when, in August 2007, I proudly announce to my father-in-law that I am about to accept an offer to join a rapidly expanding international bank in London, this beacon of common sense, responsibility, financial prudence and career stability is understandably supportive. I passionately affirm that we are finally going to stand on our own metaphorical feet financially. I reassure him that though this career move is not really about money, the reality is that I'll be getting a decent, regular wage on the 30th of each month and that he no longer needs to worry; we'll be able to start making a dent in the mortgage, paying for the kids' education and affording our own biannual plane tickets to South Africa. I'm 36 years old at the time, and we both seem to sense that I've finally arrived as a man.

Now here I am, six years later, having just been told I was being made redundant, the phone in my hand, the cat got my tongue. What am I supposed to say to Barry? How do I tell him the news? Never mind that we haven't put one penny more into the mortgage. Never mind that I owe him £4,000 for our most recent family visit to South Africa.

(Do you have any idea what it costs to fly a family of eight half way across the world? Surely the large airlines should offer discounts for taking up all those seats and oxygen on the plane?) How do I begin to explain that I no longer have a job? How do I broach a subject which carries such a deliberate implication that is blindingly obvious to both of us; that at the age of 65, when Barry should be seriously contemplating retirement after a lifetime of hard work, he feels that the eight of us are more dependent on him than ever before.

So now you know the background, perhaps you'll be more forgiving of my spinelessness and understand what I mean when I say that bumping unarmed on foot into a herd of breeding buffalo (that actually happened to me once; you'll have to wait until later for that story) felt preferable at that moment to making this phone call. Tanya's close friend Hannah refers to me as an alpha male, though I think I'm flattered by comparison to her ex-husband, whose history of fiscal irresponsibility makes me look like Warren Buffet on steroids. Misnomer or not, the reference is helpful now – I can no longer delay the inevitable. It's time to man up.

Barry picks up after the third ring. I imagine his fast receding hairline with tufts of grey at the sides, portly frame and bespectacled, thoughtful face hunched over his desk as he sifts methodically through a waft of documents pertaining to the operational and legal risk for the large international insurance company where he holds a senior executive position.

"Hello, Barry speaking," he answers sharply. Phone-speak has never really been his thing. He's a no-nonsense businessman with a sharp mind, full of common sense and witty - or at least they are in his mind - jokes. This conversation ain't gonna be easy.

"Hi Barry," I begin. I've always been very smooth with my opening lines, especially at the outset of tough conversations. "Um, I've got something I need to discuss with you. Have you got a couple of minutes?"

He hasn't even responded before I begin to choke up. This is like the other night all over again, except now I'm speaking long distance to a busy man at his place of work, not his daughter in our bedroom, tenderly soothing me while I blubber all over the duvet. "Keep it together", I scold myself. "You owe him that at least."

Barry listens as best he can, trying not to interrupt while I talk him through what has happened. When I stop, he immediately goes into practical mode, doing what he does best – risk mitigation. He asks questions about the potential severance package, the size of our mortgage, any other existing debts. He expresses residual anger towards the bank, speculating some sinister reasons behind the decision. Mr. Emotional he is not. But as the conversation draws to a close, he offers the following, as he always has done; "Brian, just know that Barb and I will do everything we can to support you all."

I pause, unable to respond immediately. Another wave of emotion washes over me, and I wait for it to pass before I speak. I am deeply touched by these few words. Barry *has* always been there for us, and though his idea of support has sometimes differed from the version Tanya and I have sought, that doesn't matter right now. What he is saying, in his own way, is that he cares and he wants to help. I know how hard this is for him and I feel desperate for having to convey this news. But he's Tanya's father, the grandfather of our six sons. We may be very different, but what we share is our love for the same people. I know Barry will be there as best as he can, and for that I am deeply grateful. It's about the most an unemployed son-in-law can expect – and wish for.

"Thank you Barry", I say. "That means a lot to us."

And it does.

I put the phone down and find myself reflecting on why this call was so difficult. Obviously, at one level, I feel terrible about the financial burden Barry feels he now needs to bear (he doesn't, but that's his stuff and his script and I ain't going to change it now). There is also the shame I feel in having to tell my father-in-law that I am out of work; that the big City job didn't quite work out as we had all hoped. This is not easy and carries with it some difficult feelings that I am unable to articulate to Barry. But I have disappointed him before and got over it. Moreover, I, we, have made choices and decisions before that he has not necessarily supported or agreed with. Since when has pleasing Barry, or to put in inversely, not disappointing him, been such an emotionally charged issue for me?

And then it becomes clear to me why I feel weepier than a guest on Oprah. It's not Barry that I really feel so bad about (if you're reading this Barry, please don't take it the wrong way and withhold your contribution towards the next Bar Mitzvah). It's me. And here, in a somewhat roundabout way, is my understanding of why.

By the beginning of 2010, a veteran of four London Marathons already, I decided it was time to have one more crack. But to do so required an extra level of motivation – a goal that would justify all the hours of training, hard work, iPod playlist selecting and carbo-loading. The target; to go sub-four hours. That would be a real push, as it would mean shaving a mere 42 minutes off my best time and require me to finish ahead of approximately ten thousand more runners than I had previously. But having run a 1;41 half marathon with Tanya that past autumn, I knew it was within me. I just needed a good training partner who would be up for a sub-four marathon, and to pray that my knees would hold up.

By now you might be wondering why I didn't select Tanya as said training partner. Well, in spite of our past differences on the road, I would have. But she had decided that the responsibilities of being a full time mother to a large family while simultaneously holding down a demanding job meant that finding the time to train for another marathon was a luxury she could not afford; that, and the suspicion - at least in my mind - that she wouldn't be able to keep up with me this time round. (I had just started on a new, secret energy drink which I was sure would give me an unbeatable advantage if it ever came down to a sprint finish between us.) Not to fear; enter Jonny, an old friend from South Africa who lived up the road in Edgware.

Jonny was a novice runner making his debut marathon, so I had my doubts as to his suitability. On the negative side, he was raw and inexperienced. On the plus side, he had the perfect runner's physique – long legs and sleek torso – and was also highly motivated by the sub-four hour target. His six foot plus frame put me at a severe disadvantage; every two of his strides were equivalent to three of mine; in my twisted mind, I was effectively running a third further. Thus, I briefly considered other options, but when Paula Radcliffe announced she was withdrawing through injury (again), I realised I should probably swallow my pride and train with Jonny.

Big mistake; never mind that with his perfectly manicured light brown hair, chiselled face and well-proportioned physique, I felt a bit like Danny de Vito running next to Arnold Schwarzenegger. More worryingly (with apologies to *The Terminator*,) the guy was a machine. He never got tired, never needed to drink, and never complained. This was like running with a male version of Tanya, a situation that was compounded when Tanya actually decided to join us on a couple of our longer training runs. But being the survivor that I am, I hung in there, and even managed to teach the young upstart a thing or two about pacing, hydration and the difference between short term dynamic psychotherapy and cognitive behavioural therapy (you find the most inane things to discuss when you spend so much time out on the road together.)

We trained hard and planned well. I was in pristine shape – or at least as good as could be expected of a 39 year old Jewish male with a fondness for gefilte fish. (If you don't know what that is, many would suggest you're missing very little.) Come Marathon day, we were all set to go; we were completely prepared, physically and mentally, to achieve our target. Our strategy for achieving sub-four was laid out; we'd be looking at running just under nine minute miles, with the aim of coming through half-way in slightly over 1;50. That would give us a small cushion if we started to tire on the back half, a concern I particularly held for Jonny as he was heading into the unknown in terms of the farthest distance he'd ever run. Nonetheless, I was confident that my far greater experience would count for a lot as the going got tough over the final few miles.

April 25th, 2010, was a glorious spring day; the course immaculately prepared to take in most of London's famous sites. The crowd was brilliant as always, the competitors in great cheer, the fancy dress costumes as outrageous as ever. We cruised past Cutty Sark and went through halfway comfortably on pace. The noise from thousands of cheering supporters at Tower Bridge was deafening. (Having my name printed on the front of my shirt boosted my confidence enormously; I hadn't heard so many people shout "Go Brian" since I was kicked out of chemistry class when I was fifteen for mixing the wrong compounds and almost blowing up the school.) At eighteen miles, things were looking good. We were on target for a reasonably comfortable sub-four; I was even starting to dream that 3;45 might be within reach if Jonny could step it up. Until that point, my biggest concern had been spotting Tanya and the Boys, who had come down to support us. Problem was, so had half a million other people and we were finding it difficult to see them in the mass of humanity. But I didn't want not finding them to be a distraction, so I put such thoughts out of my mind and stayed focussed.

Then, with about six miles to go, just as we were coming out of Docklands, something bad happened. Not to Jonny, but to me. I got tired. I don't mean a little fatigued, slightly pooped or in need of a quick nap. I mean dead tired, like completely finished. I felt I couldn't take another step. The blistering early pace had taken its toll. I had also made the rookie mistake of not fuelling enough in the first half of the race (who's the novice now, hotshot?) I was desperately close to hitting the proverbial wall. We were in trouble. And so was the sub-four hour target.

I tried everything. I envisaged positive thoughts; I fast forwarded to Leona Lewis' ridiculously appropriate *Run* on my iPod; I poured Lucozade down my throat and ibuprofen gel all over my legs. I even imagined it was

Tanya goading me on, not Jonny. But nothing was working. I had slowed to a virtual walk, and could barely put one leg in front of the other.

"Come on Brian," Jonny cajoled me.

"I can't," I replied through gritted teeth.

"Come on Brian," screamed about 78,000 other strangers in encouragement (man, I was regretting having printed my name on my shirt now.)

"I can't," I replied to no one in particular. This was getting silly.

I pulled to the side and put Leona on pause. "Jon, listen man. You've got to push on. I can't do it. If you hang here with me, you may not make sub-four. Just go. I'll see you at the finish."

Jonny's answer was instantaneous. "No."

"Go."

"No".

"Go."

This rhyming argument in front of 78 000 people who really didn't know me that well was getting ridiculous, especially as we had just been passed by a 69 year old grandmother dressed as a Mars Bar.

"Jon," I implored one last time. "You've trained so hard for this. Just because I've slowed down, doesn't mean you have to. Come on, push ahead and at least one of us will make our time."

Jonny looked me square in the eyes. "Listen Bri, I'm not leaving you. We're in this together. If we make sub-four, then great. And if not, that's also cool. End of story."

And with that, my friend gave me a little nudge and gently started to amble ahead, looking behind to ensure I was following. Which I did – very slowly.

Out there on the streets of London before countless spectators and thousands of fellow runners, Jonny bestowed on me a great kindness and helped me learn a most profound lesson. We had trained for this race for over five months. We had run hundreds of miles, constantly planning and plotting our strategy for finishing in less than four hours. We had talked tactics and pacing; we had it all worked out. That was our goal; it was why we were running this thing. Running 26 miles in less than four hours really mattered to us both. And then, when that goal was placed in serious jeopardy by my body's malfunctioning, my friend did a remarkable thing. He let go. Just like that.

And in case you were wondering, the next six miles were sheer torture. I hobbled and shuffled, through the cobbles, down Victoria Embankment and up past Westminster. I turned onto Birdcage Walk, barely moving as we passed Big Ben. Jonny stayed with me the whole way, supporting, encouraging, carrying me mentally and virtually physically. And as we staggered into the home straight which is The Mall, passing Buckingham Palace on our left as we did so, I looked up at the giant clock suspended above the finish line, not a hundred yards away. We were going to make it. Seconds later, we crossed the threshold together. Time; 3 hours and 57 minutes. Even though Jonny had let go six miles previously, we had somehow managed to make sub-four.

What's all this got to do with my redundancy story? Well, what Jonny taught me with this whole *letting go* thing, was the sheer power and control that our thinking holds over us. I've come to realise that my decision to do an MBA a number of years back, which would serve as the catalyst for my major career shift, was predicated on some thinking that I had been holding onto for some time. This thinking had really begun to matter to me and could be summed up in one word; responsibility.

Now it may seem strange to hear a guy who had been working for ten years in the charity sector talking about responsibility – I mean hey, that was the buzzword in the environment within which I worked. Taking responsibility for others, for the community, for the world – this was the currency that motivated us all. But I'm talking about a different kind of responsibility, the kind that is more deeply personal. I had decided it was time to become more responsible for my family and myself – or at least to attach a new meaning to what this idea meant to me.

Listen to the stories I started telling myself; I believed (and had been repeatedly told) that my background and upbringing had 'high achiever' written all over it, so it was time to receive a consistent, predictable income that was an appropriate reflection of my education, age and capabilities. It was time to start building my career in a more linear way, pursuing a clearer trajectory. It was time to go into the 'real world' where I could apply my mind and pit my wits against other people of similar ambition. It was time to achieve my potential, to gain appropriate levels of recognition in the eyes of others, to do what I should be doing in the world. In short, it was time to pursue relentlessly my recently updated version of being responsible.

Armed with my new-found beliefs, I embarked on my new life in the City and did exactly that. I behaved, for the most part, responsibly. (The time when I made a 'business' trip to the Manchester office on the same day United were at home to Chelsea was an exception I am not entirely proud of.) I made responsible decisions about my career, my family and my choice of breakfast cereals. So there I was – Mr. Responsible, a source of pride to my mother, my father-in-law, my barber and my community. I still didn't have any money in the bank account at the end of the month, but at least the possibility existed that I might. I was pretty much there.

Of course, this was all based on the perception I had created for myself – and had allowed others to help craft for me. Consequently, my version of making responsible choices had been framed by the image I, and a whole lot of other people, had constructed. There was nothing necessarily wrong with that image; it's just that it wasn't necessarily me.

When faced with thinking we take seriously, most people find it very hard to let go. The very intensity of our thinking is what makes us highly invested in it; we confuse a thought with a fact and assume that the way we are looking at the world is the only way to do so. Letting go of that requires openness, courage and an understanding that our thoughts, even when they matter a lot to us, are just that – thoughts. In my case, I had convinced myself that my understanding of the notion of responsibility had become a fact – an absolute reality that underpinned so many significant life decisions that followed and which consumed me in my relentless, and ultimately futile pursuit, of its realisation.

By now it should be obvious why the call to Barry had been so distressing to me. I didn't have a job anymore, so clearly the whole responsibility thing hadn't worked out too well. Admitting that to my father-in-law was hard enough. Admitting it to myself was nearly impossible. I had made being responsible the Holy Grail; only to discover that it was elusive as ever. It had become a fixation in my mind, a necessary requirement for the life I wanted to live. I had taken my personal thinking very seriously – way too seriously as it turned out. I had failed in the one thing I had set out to achieve. I felt utterly bereft.

Looking back now, this is what Jonny taught me when he let go of the 'sub-four hour thought' in the midst of the 2010 London Marathon. Sub-four was a great target and a highly motivating goal. It mattered to us – but it *wasn't* the Holy Grail. It was just a good thing to aim for. The question was; could I reframe the notion of responsibility in my own mind with the kind of grace and equanimity that Jonny had found at the twenty mile mark?

I had arrived at a seminal moment. Being made redundant had brought me, in Tony's words, to my 'inflection point.' I needed to find the courage to ask myself some really important questions; could I let go of my notion of responsibility? Could I let go of other core beliefs and thinking that I held so dear? Could I let go of my version of the sub-four hour target?

And as much as I was hurting, I was slowly beginning to feel the stirrings of the humility and self honesty that would be required if I was willing to ask myself the toughest of all questions; could I let go of this account of my journey that I had convinced myself, for so long, must be the right one for me?

II

Perspective through Humility

Be exceedingly humble in spirit, for the anticipated end of mortal man is worms.
Ethics of the Fathers

6. To move on

Resentment is like drinking poison and then waiting for your enemy to kill you.
Nelson Mandela

May 25th
As part of the prescribed process, another meeting was scheduled for Friday morning, three days after the initial 'discussion' with Craig and Lauren. It was 10;31 am and we were settled around a small table in a private meeting room on the sixth floor of the London headquarters of SKBK Bank.

"Listen Brian, this has got to be one of the hardest things I've had to do," Craig began. I looked into his eyes and a part of me really believed what he was saying. It was obvious that this was not easy for him. This wasn't some guy from HR reading out a corporate memo he had been asked to recite on behalf of some faceless executive. This was a real human being who took his leadership responsibilities seriously and who was grappling with delivering a difficult and painful message. If you really want to know the truth, and as much as I'd like to characterise him differently, Craig was a decent man who was just doing what he thought was right. Sure, it would be easy for me to paint him as a power-fuelled, narcissistic autocrat, dispensing with people's heads like Henry the Eighth. But that wouldn't be fair on him.

On the other hand, don't feel the need to weep too much for Craig. After all, this was ultimately his decision and his message. Whatever our good history and previous relationship, it wasn't going to stop him making what he thought was the right call for the business. While Craig had a reputation for playing hard yet fair, I'd also seen him make some questionable personnel calls over the years, especially when it involved circumventing the normal process in order to expedite a desired outcome. In other words, if he wanted you out, you were out. In my particular case, I was exposed and vulnerable. My main backer had left and unlike the others, I didn't have a business line producing revenues to act as a buffer.

While Craig spoke, my mind wondered to events of the past couple of days. I had been encouraged by Lauren to bring someone along, either within the organisation or external to it, in order to offer support. I briefly considering inviting Bill – a friend of mine from the gym who works as a school teacher by day and moonlights as a professional wrestler by night (you'd never recognise him, as he wrestles under a mask with the Mexican pseudonym El Gigante) – but wisely decided against it. Although his cobra clutch finishing manoeuvre has been known to reduce 400 pound men to tears within 3.7 seconds, I chose on reflection to go with a slightly more subtle, cerebral approach. So instead I asked Professor Malcolm Rochester, a former colleague in the Organisational Effectiveness team, to accompany me.

Malcolm, or Prof as I liked to call him, was a man in his late fifties who possessed a head full of grey hair that sat atop a stocky build. His sharp eyes and wizened face hinted at his genuine intelligence and considerable life experience. He was a man of purpose and conviction. A former provincial squash player, he walked around the building quicker than anyone I'd ever met. Yet he had a side to his personality that I sometimes found difficult to figure out. He was intensely private and very guarded regarding his personal life, rarely making reference to his wife and children. It made for an interesting contrast to my much more outgoing, open style. As members of the OE team, we had worked closely together for a number of years, partnering with each other in our consulting role to the Investment and Commercial Banking business.

Prof and I made a good team. His broad experience, insight and considered way complemented my more forthright manner and commercially oriented approach. We were perceived as a partnership that served the business effectively; Frank de Angelo, who ran our Residential Mortgages business and sat two desks away from me, referred to us collectively as the 'Professor and the Priest'. Although I was more rabbi than Christian clergyman, the joint pseudonym was both humorous and appreciated – it affectionately described collaboration that while not quite made in heaven (the religious references notwithstanding), was an effective and focussed combination of skills and personality.

Nonetheless, our association was ultimately unable to withstand one of the most significant differences between us, which manifested in the different ways we addressed our career ambitions. Prof, despite his piercing intellect, vast experience and extensive array of higher education qualifications, had chosen to follow what I sometimes thought of as the path of least resistance. He avoided taking major risks, both personally and professionally. Although this often meant restraining himself and his undoubted capabilities, it was a call he made in the interests of his own piece of mind and longevity within the organisation. He had turned his back on a highly distinguished academic career to join the Bank. Despite his age, he had two relatively young children to support and having made a significant career shift late in life, Prof wasn't about to rock the boat too much.

And therein lay the primary difference between us. I, at a very different stage of life, became increasingly eager to hive off in a different direction. Having worked closely with the senior guys within the ICB business, I began to want a piece of that action; I no longer felt satisfied with what I perceived to be a consulting role on the periphery. I wanted to be at the heart of things, to apply my mind and skills to shape and drive the business forward. Having established myself and my credibility within the Bank, my self-image had shifted into overdrive. The grandiose aspirations and drives – money, status, sitting at the top table, making an impact - were all accessible to me if only I could secure a more senior position in the business. Or at least that was the illusion under which I was labouring.

So when Tony came calling almost five years into my time at the Bank with the Strategy role, it suited my ambitions and self-perception perfectly. I leapt enthusiastically at the opportunity to move from consulting into the business unit proper. In so doing, I brought a quick dissolution to my partnership with Malcolm and replaced it with a not-so-subtle tension; for while Prof Rochester restrained himself and his ambitions, I did the opposite. Mine developed unbridled, and as that became increasingly clear to us both, a distance between us began to emerge. The relentless pursuit of my ambition had become an almost over-powering force.

But when the redundancy process was thrust upon me and as I became painfully aware that my ambitions had not only been thwarted, but that my entire career had been put on hold, I turned to Prof Malcolm for help. I'm not sure if I would have had the humility or the desire to make contact, but when my former colleague reached out via email, offering his support, I responded positively.

In preparation, Malcolm and I had met the day prior to the second Craig and Lauren meeting, in Artisan, a trendy organic coffee shop under the shadow of St. Paul's, where Malcolm reassured me that most of the senior members of the Exco had fought to reverse Craig's decision. He said that a number of the guys had really gone to bat for me, suggesting that the Strategy role be re-shaped in a way that would better suit the new leadership style. When that was rejected, others had proposed extending the time frame, so as to allow the new management team time to settle in before making any knee-jerk decisions about my future. Another argument put forward was that the new divisional head would benefit from having me around to support him as the business underwent a significant restructure. But ultimately, it seems as if Craig's mind was made up already. The powers that be had determined that it was time for a change, and my association with the previous regime seemed to make my position untenable in their eyes.

Prof helped me to see that the process around which the decision on my redundancy had been taken was somewhat flawed. I was grateful for his input, as it helped to crystallise my own thinking. I was not in a position to reverse the decision; that was clear. I realised rather that my objections lay not with the actual decision itself, but with the speed with which it was taken, and the insufficient consultation around it, especially considering the positive support and feedback I was receiving from my executive colleagues. As a reasonably senior guy myself, who had been around a while and worked hard to live the company's values and culture, I felt I deserved better. The firm had always stressed its commitment to treating people as adults, yet I had felt infantilised the moment Lauren walked into Room 105 holding that envelope. Things had happened too fast. I had been told my role was redundant; thereafter, everything else was merely the process by which that decision was executed. Perhaps in the big shops that was common place, but in SKBK Bank, I expected more.

As Malcolm and I spoke this through, he offered his unique blend of practical advice and wise insight. He helped me craft an approach to the following day's meeting, affirming my desire to handle matters in as non-confrontational and dispassionate a way as I could muster. He encouraged me to think about other options within the Bank; he went as far to wonder whether I would consider relocating to our Toronto office to take a hands-on role in developing the business over there. But though the idea of going back to live and work just down the road from where I had been born and brought up had its nostalgic appeal, the fact that none of my six kids could skate or ski quickly ruled that one out. Prof was doing his job well and I asked him if he would be by my side for the next stage of the process, though knowing his propensity for placating rather than openly challenging leadership, I was uncertain if he would stand tall when I really needed him.

Now, as I listened to Craig reiterating the reasons behind the redundancy, it became clear that I was pretty much on my own. So when Craig paused for a moment, I jumped straight in.

"Look guys," I said in my most conciliatory voice – the one I use when trying to explain to Tanya why I neglected to pick up the dry cleaning on the way home. "I'm not going to try and reverse your decision. I think I understand your rationale, and it kind of makes sense – at least I can see it from your perspective."

For a moment, I thought one of them might be about to nominate me for a Nobel Peace Prize. I quickly undermined that possibility with my next comment.

"But I do feel that this has not been handled very well. We've all known each other a long time. You know I'm not a risk to the business, whatever happens. I've always tried to be a good citizen, and I think you understand that."

Craig held my gaze, giving nothing away. He had clearly prepared himself mentally for this meeting – his position had been established and was not subject to negotiation. To my left, Prof remained silent. I needed him now, but he wasn't stepping up.

Turning towards Lauren, I ploughed ahead. "I don't think this whole situation has been managed appropriately or is reflective of our culture. No disrespect Lauren, but I would have appreciated first having a proper discussion with Craig about it, without the formal HR intervention, even if the final decision is not subject to review. I feel I deserved that at least."

There went that Nobel Prize. Oh well, at least I still had my health.

I had really hoped Prof would weigh in a bit on my behalf, but he seemed content to merely implicitly endorse what I was saying, rather than assertively remind everyone of the support that had been received from others or the flawed process that we had discussed the day before. But I guess I should have known better; that was not Malcolm's way. As a fundamentally risk-averse person who had long ago learned to keep his aspirations and ambitions in check, he wasn't going to change now or put his neck on the line, not for me at least.

I rambled on a bit longer, re-iterating my position from different perspectives, until I had virtually exhausted myself. I was running out of energy and inclination fast – as were the others. There was an inevitability about the whole process that smacked of a kind of legalistic disingenuousness. So looking Craig directly in the eye, I fired my final salvo; "I've done my job Craig, and based on all the feedback I've received, I've done it well. You may not have agreed with this role in the first place – fair enough – but I've only done what was asked of me. It's unfortunate that wasn't taken into account."

Perhaps because there was some truth in what I was saying, Craig and Lauren listened and did not object or try and defend how the process had played out. Yet I couldn't help but feel that by letting me vent, they were playing it smart. Rather than engaging in what could have been a destructive or confrontational conversation, they accepted my feedback without protest. I was discovering that it's extremely hard to have a fight with yourself. (If you don't believe me, try it sometime.) Of course, it all didn't matter anyway. I was on my way out; now they just needed to see it through.

My mini-tirade over, Lauren carefully explained the process over the next two weeks, during which I was free to pursue any opportunity in the Bank that might be of interest. She ran me through some of the practicalities of the next fortnight, stressing that I could come and go as I pleased and set up any internal meetings that might be helpful to me. This was a relief and helped to dispel images I had conjured up of being frog-marched out of the building while somebody retrieved my valuables from my desk. On the other hand, I was to disengage immediately from the various initiatives and strategic projects I had been working on; so that was it for me and North American expansion - no more baseball and beer. And somebody else would now be entrusted with running the various committees I had been managing, while building our team in the Channel Islands would be handled by Craig himself from now on. We briefly talked about some high level numbers - Craig generously stated that "we'll take care of you through the transition." It could have been construed as being slightly patronising or a way of assuaging his - or the organisation's conscience - but I wasn't about to object. This wasn't exactly Custer's last stand, but I had said what I needed to say it, and felt better for it (at least for the next thirty seconds or so.)

The meeting came to a reasonably amicable end. I had been hoping, somewhat perversely, for more of an animated response from the others. But they weren't up for it - or more accurately - they didn't need to be. They were well within their legal rights to proceed with the redundancy and the absence of meaningful conversation around the decision either hadn't occurred to them, or they had chosen to ignore the need for it. Either way, it didn't matter. They held all the cards and all I could do was play the hand I'd been dealt.

For a moment, I re-considered calling Bill and asking him to meet me in the Exec car park with his El Gigante mask, but then I remembered that he was on a school trip – or a wrestling tour of the Middle East – I can't recall which.

So I calmed myself down, thanked the guys for listening and headed for the lift. There was nothing more to be said. The two week clock had started ticking; my redundancy was now in full swing and from here on in, it was just a matter of time before we all said goodbye for good.

I think it's fair to say that most people in my situation would have been pretty agitated, to put it mildly. There were a fair number of legitimate reasons to be angry, and several people to whom I could have chosen to direct that anger. I had done nothing wrong and a fair bit right. As I have repeated somewhat obsessively, and will do so again here, since I'm only human, this redundancy seemed to have nothing to do with my performance. As Craig himself put it right at the beginning; "You've been caught in the middle of something entirely not of your own making."

I didn't exactly have a reputation for being a pushover; actually, I've never been very good at accepting difficult things with great equanimity. If anything, I'm often fuelled by a sense of righteous indignation, as my friend Jack calls it, which motivates me to fight a perceived injustice, especially when it pertains to me. So where did my relatively benign acceptance of this all come from? After all, it would have been perfectly natural and understandable to express anger towards some of the key people behind the decision to make me redundant. Where was it? Since when had I transformed myself from Donald Trump to Mother Theresa?

Well, to be completely frank, I hadn't. Of course there were certain individuals whom I felt had not done right by me. There were definitely fleeting moments of malice and ill will which I did not deny myself and actually quite enjoyed. And certainly I was experiencing perfectly natural feelings of hurt and shock; it would be naive to imagine that I did not know who had been the cause. No, Mother Theresa I was not (though I'm grateful for the comparison.)

Yet it's also true that I did not struggle with deep feelings of resentment or bitterness. I had my moments, sure, but there was no dart board in my kid's bedroom with pictures of Craig, Rupert or Russell Brand on it (though there should have been – at least in Russell's case.) Even as I walked out of that building in the immediate aftermath of a meeting that could be construed as a set-up from the moment it started, with me as the fall guy, I found myself able to move on relatively easily, particularly from those most responsible for my plight.

How? Why?

For the first twelve years of my life, my dad was pretty much as good a dad as you find anywhere. There were some obvious weaknesses – almost all related to his lack of sporting prowess – but they were easy to overlook when taking a holistic view of the man, even through the eyes of a young boy. My father had a wonderful mix of traits; he was thoughtful, compassionate, empathic, and slow to anger; provided the right balance of praise, encouragement and guidance. He was also brilliant, but not in a mad scientist kind of way. He had an innate wisdom about him that was completely congruent with his quiet and humble manner, and a capacity for insight that made him perfectly suited to being the outstanding psychiatrist that he was. He was extremely highly regarded by his peers, respected in the community, adored by many of his patients and loved by his immediate family – my mother, sister and me. He was a good man and a great dad.

Values mattered to my father a great deal. He abhorred prejudice of any form – from an early age, treating all people with equal dignity, respect and consideration was instilled into my sister and me. He wasn't big on pronouncements or asserting his moral and parental authority, but when he felt strongly about something, he didn't hold back. One of the only times I can recall my father striking me occurred when I was eleven years old; I was watching cricket on TV when I noticed some spectators spilling onto the pitch. As they swarmed across the playing field, I used a derogatory term to describe the skin colour of the pitch invaders – a term whose meaning I didn't know, but had heard being used on the school playground. I suddenly felt a hard slap across my naked cheek. Momentarily stunned, I looked up to see my father's face glowering at me.

"No child of mine will ever use that kind of language. We don't speak like that about anyone. Understand?"

Through glistening eyes, I nodded. He was neither a violent nor angry man, so if he felt this strongly about something, it clearly mattered. Lesson learned; *to this day.*

These values, and my parents' deep commitment to them, were a primary catalyst in their decision to leave South Africa in the late 60's shortly after my sister Karen was born. This was a dark time in South Africa's history, as the entrenched Nationalist government was promulgating its vicious Apartheid policies with impunity. For liberal white South Africans, being part of this perverse society had an insidious and deeply disturbing effect. To stay, and to remain silent to the gross injustice, meant to benefit, either directly or indirectly, from the outrage being perpetuated on the millions of non-whites who constituted the vast majority of the population. But to openly object meant almost certain persecution by the state security forces and likely imprisonment. My parents, like a small minority of like-minded people in the country at the time, felt trapped by the moral implications of remaining part of a society that had become a pariah in the eyes of the rest of the world. So when my father received an opportunity to specialise in psychiatry at the esteemed McMaster University in the little known steel town of Hamilton, Ontario, not far from the Canadian-American border, it offered a way of resolving this dilemma. He and my mother decided it was time to leave.

I was born in Hamilton not long after they arrived. In the meantime, my father's career progressed quickly, so that the building of a picturesque family home in the quaint, peaceful little suburb of Dundas on the outskirts of town was the next logical step. In no time at all, as a young boy flourishing on the idyllic suburban streets, I had become the epitome of the all-Canadian kid.

Dad was a key part of that very happy childhood. I don't really remember too many specifics but maybe that's the point; there are no negative memories from this period of my life. Dad was just there, schlepping me to my ice hockey games, carting me around when I broke my leg playing Canadian football and commiserating with me when we had to give away our first dog Muffin for repeatedly biting the postman. (In hindsight, the dog was probably demonstrating perfectly natural passive-aggressive tendencies in response to being saddled with such a naff name.) Dad was doing what good Dads do best; helping to create an environment in which I felt safe, secure and loved. I couldn't have asked for more - until it all came to a shuddering halt.

It was early one weekday evening; Dad had come home from work earlier than usual. We were sitting round the kitchen table. Something wasn't right; we could sense it in the air and see it in their slightly reddened eyes.

"Kids, do you know what it means when parents get a divorce?" Dad asked softly.

I was eleven, Karen thirteen. We both nodded.

"Well, Mommy and I getting a divorce. This has got absolutely nothing to do with you; it's not your fault in any way. We love you very much and would never want to hurt either of you. But this is something we have to do."

Dad stopped for a moment and seemed to be struggling with he wanted to say next.

"This is definitely not your mother's fault, so don't blame her. Mommy and I still love each other very much, but not in the way that we used to. This is going to be hard on all of us, especially the two of you. I'm so, so sorry..."

Dad couldn't finish his sentence. He began to cry – the first time I think I had ever seen him weep – and Mom took over. I remember nothing more of that conversation, but the image of the pain and sadness and tears etched on his face that day is forever seared into my memory. Dad had alluded that the cause of the marriage break-up was his, but it would take years before I arrived at an inkling of what was behind his inescapable anguish.

The next day, Dad moved out. And so, life changed radically for us. Of course, it is important not to be too melodramatic here; millions of kids every year around the world experience a similar fate. And we were still incredibly fortunate – we had a loving, caring mother and father who would do all they could for us - it's just that they would not do it together anymore. I guess what made it particularly impacting in our case was the sheer contrast of it all. Life had been good; too good to be true as it turned out. The abrupt and extreme nature of the change would make this transition very difficult for both my sister and me. Things would definitely be different from now on and the idyllic life of the all-Canadian kid was no more.

Not surprisingly, things changed pretty drastically and quickly after that conversation around the kitchen table. Within a few months we would be uprooted from Canada and on our way back to South Africa – all four of us still in the same country, but no longer under the same roof. For our sake and hers, my mother had wanted to be near her parents whose home was in Johannesburg. My grandparents were wonderful, warm, caring people – a beacon of stability, emotional consistency and unconditional love that would play a crucial role during such a tumultuous period in all our lives.

But there was another, more sinister reason for our returning to the country my parents had so boldly left almost fifteen years before. There was another person involved, whom my father had met on a recent visit to South Africa. We had come back so he could be with that person – this was where my father wanted to be. And it was around then we noticed he was beginning to change.

The differences that I saw in my Dad didn't occur overnight; he did not suddenly become an uncaring, disengaged parent. And of course, as I was maturing and approaching adolescence, I was starting to see him and others (not to mention the newly discovered spots on my face) in a new light anyway. But pimples or no pimples, Dad had changed; he seemed more pre-occupied with his own life and his private and emotional needs; ours sometimes felt as if they had become lost amidst his own considerations. Dad became increasingly moody and fractious; his once calm temperament struggled to assert itself, hinting at the deeper inner turmoil that threatened to embroil him.

In the good ole Dundas days, Dad (and Mom of course) had always made me feel – without my ever being aware of it – as if their life revolved around mine. Not anymore. Now, my life had to fit into Dad's. I had to do what he wanted to do, sleep at his place when it suited him, go on holiday to the places he wished to visit. I had to spend time with the people of his choosing, in the environment he chose. I was desperate for him to come and watch me play my newly discovered South African sports like rugby and cricket, but he rarely showed up. Instead, I felt pressured to accompany him to the things he enjoyed – opera, ballet, film festivals. Not exactly the bread and butter of your average teenage boy.

But worst of all, Dad insisted on us building and developing a relationship with the new person in his life. We felt pressured into accepting and responding to someone who we had no good feelings towards, whom quite simply, we didn't like. Yet our reluctance was not subject to discussion or exploration. Dad wanted it to be a certain way, and we were too young, too vulnerable and too powerless in the face of his insistence to offer any resistance.

Of course he still looked out for us, never abrogating his responsibility and always doing his best to make decisions that were in our interest. We knew he still loved us in the way only a father could. He hadn't become a bad Dad, but here comes the really hard part; this was a version of Dad that we didn't particularly like much of the time.

Almost unavoidably, as I grew older, if not wiser, the distance between my father and me widened. And although I didn't fully understand it at the time, I was beginning to grapple with some very difficult and deep feelings towards one of the two people who loved me most in the world. I was becoming angry with my father. Soon, as so often happens, that anger transformed itself into one of the most insidious forces that I believe a human being can experience – resentment.

Fortunately, the resentment did not consume me. I was more or less able to get on with my life; I met Tanya in my early twenties, fell in love and got engaged, began planning our immigration to Israel, became a religious fanatic, dreamt of building my own family in the way that made sense to me, and then fell in love with Tanya properly. Life wasn't always easy, but I felt I had moved on and was doing okay. But the resentment never left me; I just managed to keep it locked in a place in my heart that didn't seem to do me, or others, much harm.

Then Dad fell ill. Actually, he'd been ill for a while but had kept it from us for as long as he could. But when he started losing weight at an alarming pace, he could not keep the secret any longer. He deteriorated so quickly that we even considered bringing the wedding forward (not easy when your engagement is only three months long in the first place). Dad was dying. It wasn't the big 'C', or another illness that, no matter how terrible, did not carry with it the social stigma or psychological burden that this one did, especially in conservative South Africa in the mid 1990's. Dad had AIDS.

In the days before anti-retro viral drugs became readily available, AIDS, or more accurately HIV, was an incurable disease. Dad's headlong descent into death could not be halted; only delayed. We watched helplessly as his condition deteriorated rapidly; he lost more and more weight, becoming increasingly weak and unable to stave off the infections that would ultimately kill him. He suffered terribly; from chronic diarrhoea, acute nausea, unremitting vomiting and many other ailments that we were often unaware of since he strove to keep them to himself. He rarely complained; suffering for the most part in relative silence.

As he lay in a private ward of a Johannesburg hospital, Dad's condition continued to decline. The end lurched quickly closer. Yet he clung on. Dad wasn't ready to let go, to say goodbye to the people he loved. His body was preparing to leave this world, but his heart and soul were not yet in alignment. There was one more person whom he still needed to see, perhaps to make some kind of final amends, before he was ready to depart.

My mother, who had remarried when I was seventeen, was travelling overseas with my step-father during the period in which Dad had been hospitalised. He was now down to his final days, unable to move from his bed, virtually unable to speak. But we knew he wanted to see Mom, with whom he had managed to retain a loving and deeply respectful relationship despite all that had occurred so many years ago. And Mom wanted to see Dad. So as soon as she landed, she rushed straight from the airport to his bedside at the hospital. Leaning down, she took his hand in hers. Dad's eyes were closed; he could no longer see.

"Julian," Mom greeted him in such a tender voice. "It's Max. I'm here."

Dad gave Mom's hand an almost imperceptible squeeze, acknowledging her presence. He had waited for her. Now he was ready to go.

Mom and I stepped out of the room momentarily – we hadn't seen each other in months as we were living on opposite sides of the world. When we stepped back into the room moments later, Dad had stopped breathing. Too painful for him to leave while any of us were still with him in the room, Dad, left alone for the briefest of periods for the first time in days, slipped quietly away forever.

Dad's death at the age of 53 was an undoubted tragedy; the premature demise of a brilliant man with much still to contribute to the world, and much still to work through with the people he loved most. Dad passed away less than three months after the birth of his first grandchild, our eldest son Baruch; had he been alive today, 17 years later, he would have been blessed – like my mother – with 11 beautiful grandchildren. Perhaps it is purely a fantasy that sustains me, but I believe were Dad still with us, the sheer joy and pride that he would have received from his grandchildren would have brought him genuine peace and contentment in the sunset of his life. Without doubt, this thought is the greatest personal sadness of my life.

Yet still, even posthumously, I couldn't help shaking off the feelings of anger towards my father. The resentment was so deep rooted, so profound, that his passing alone would not cleanse me of it. I needed to do some work on this – to have a shift of consciousness that would free me from these feelings towards him.

It didn't happen straight away. Actually, that shift arrived unexpectedly a number of years later. I was attending a weekend seminar, an event promoting personal growth and well-being. Working with people in the not for profit sector at the time, I was looking for something that would assist me in helping others. I was also looking for something to help me – though I didn't really know it then.

I remember very little from that weekend. It was all a bit touchy-feely for an alpha male like me, even one with a psychotherapy background. They made us desist from all vices for the entire weekend – for me that amounted to no coffee and no WWE (if you don't know what that is, please don't worry) for a 48 hour period. So perhaps it was the caffeine cold turkey effect that has caused much of what they taught us to be lost in a blur.

But one thing landed, that's for sure. Pascale, the woman who was co-facilitating the seminar, spoke quietly into the microphone; "Think of someone to whom you hold resentment. It probably means that you have good reason for holding on to this in your mind. But that's not the point – it doesn't matter if these feelings are valid or not; new or old; if you've felt them for many years or more recently. Just reflect on that feeling of resentment."

I sat there somewhat dumbfounded. I didn't really do resentment. Try as I might, I couldn't come up with anyone or anything. There was some residual anger towards Chloe Orkin for beating me into second place in the high school public speaking competition three years running, but I figured that didn't really count. So I was kind of stuck. And then Pascale uttered the following final addendum to her instruction; "The person can be either alive or dead."

At the time, my father had been dead for about eight years. But the minute she added this qualification, I knew I had found my resentment. It came to me so unexpectedly that I sat stunned by the realisation. I resented Dad; *a lot.*

Pascale and her colleagues taught us something I will forever be grateful for, though in hindsight, it is so obvious it is almost embarrassing to admit. Resentment – the feeling of ill will, over an extended period of time, towards another - achieves nothing. It does not change the person towards whom you feel it. It does not change the situation. It does however change you, but only to your detriment. It costs you – big time. It eats away at you, an insidious poison from within, consuming your psychological, emotional and spiritual well-being in ways you are only peripherally aware of, if you're lucky.

And here's the real belter; resentment has nothing to do with whether there is good reason or not. As a matter of fact, as Pascale taught us, most often resentment will make perfect sense to the person holding onto it – otherwise why hold on to it so dearly in the first place? The great capacity of the human mind to rationalise – and to transform such rationalisation into the source of sustained feelings of ill will towards another – is what makes resentment such an enduring companion.

What stunned me was the awareness that I had been holding resentment towards my father for so long, right through my teenage years into my adult life, through his illness and death, until this very day. For reasons unique to our father-son relationship, I was still clinging onto my anger. At the seminar, they told us about the cost of holding onto resentment – they even encouraged us to do a kind of cost-benefit analysis; what you gain contrasted with what you lose by refusing to let go of the resentment. And I concluded that holding resentment, even unconsciously, towards my late father, was costing me a great deal.

My negative feelings towards my father and how he had handled us in the aftermath of the divorce were obfuscating other more joyful emotions and memories. These were preventing me from having a more neutral, less jaded view of a person who, for all his faults and mistakes, was fundamentally a good, kind, moral and caring human being and father. Most of the time, he had tried to do what was right; often he succeeded, sometimes he failed. The deep emotional pain Dad felt at the end of life, evidenced by the copious tears he spilled on a frequent basis, was enough for both of us for a lifetime. I did not need to add to those tears, nor prolong the pain or the sadness or the mistakes of the past any longer. Rather, I needed to find the compassion, empathy and love that his commitment as a Dad deserved. The alternative was for to me to carry on, perhaps for the rest of my life, with feelings of ill will and negative memories towards the only man who would ever love me completely and unconditionally.

I think back to the second to the last night of Dad's life. I was alone in his hospital room with him; it was late, and the ward had gone quiet save for the occasional groan of patients or the soft chatter of nurses. I was sitting quietly next to Dad's bed, when he beckoned me over; with almost the last vestige of strength, he pulled me towards him. He was already so thin, so gaunt, so pitifully weak. The powerful life-force had almost drained entirely from him; a man once so robust, so full of physical, psychological, intellectual and emotional energy was now reduced to so much less. It was desperately painful for us both.

"Brian, my Boy," he whispered ever so softly into my ear. "I want you to know something. I haven't always agreed with all the choices you've made in your life. But, I've always said that I would support you no matter what, even if I wouldn't have chosen it for you in the first ..."

An uncontrollable cough rose in his chest, halting him mid-sentence. The pneumonia that would soon end his life had embedded itself deep within his lungs. I waited for the heaving chest to subside, holding on to him helplessly.

"I ... I want you to know that I'm so proud of you, my Boy. And I want you to know, that were I to choose again, I would choose for you all that you've chosen for yourself."

That was just about the last thing my father ever said to me. And these words are the ones that I choose to hold on to and to cherish, so that I can let go. So that I can move on.

Being able to forgive my father was one of the most precious gifts I could ever have given myself. And it taught me that if I could do it with Dad, then surely I could so with others.

There is no question in my mind that the redundancy could have been handled better. There were a number of people who were culpable to varying degrees, who each played their part in a process that did not live up to the high standards the firm set for it. Sure they could have done better, but that's not the point. For this story is about me – not them. I have come to understand that the final stage of letting go of resentment is forgiveness. We all make mistakes; we all have moments when we let ourselves and others down. Learning to forgive is the only way to move on when others have hurt us in some way or another. Ultimately, I can only take responsibility for my own self – my actions, behaviour and thoughts. To dwell on who had caused me to become redundant or the way they had arrived at and implemented that decision would be of no benefit; to hold ill will towards any of them would not serve me in any way.

It took me about twenty years, many of them long after his death, for me to arrive at that insight concerning my father. But because I did so, it took me only moments to come to that same understanding with regards to my former colleagues. I would not be resentful of them because the cost was simply too high. Instead, I could move on, free of the bitterness that a part of me so badly wanted to feel.

It was only three days since that first meeting with Craig and Lauren in Room 105, but already I had started to leave the Bank behind in my mind. There would be more twists and turns in the immediate road ahead, but new dreams were emerging - of different choices, of a different life.

Dad would have understood. I even think Dad would have been proud.

7. Opening up to connection

I keep thinking we need a new kind of language, a language of the heart ... some kind of language between people that is a new kind of poetry – that is the poetry of the dancing bee that tells us where the honey is. And I think that in order to create that language we're going to have to learn how you go through a looking glass into another kind of perception, in which you have that sense of being united to all things, and suddenly you understand everything.
My Dinner with Andre

May 26th
We had come down to Brighton for the long weekend. It's funny sometimes how things work out. Here I was, a full five days after being made redundant, and we were walking along the famous Brighton pier as if we didn't have a care in the world.

The truth was, we had booked this trip months ago, when my mother and step-father Dan said they'd like us to all go away together for a few days. At the time, with a steady income, a stable career and lots of leave accumulated, it seemed like a good idea. Or at least to me and the kids it did. Tanya, not surprisingly, had her reservations. In no particular order, phrased as questions, but to the perceptive mind that is mine, understood as possible reasons not to go, they went something like this; 1) Do you have any idea how much kosher food is required to feed a family of eight – plus your Mom and Dan – for four days in Brighton? 2) Is this going to feel like a holiday for me or am I going to spend most of the time in the kitchen? 3) How do we know it's not going to rain the entire weekend? 4) Why can't we just get an extra couple of tubs of Ben & Jerry's on Sunday and take the kids to Legoland for the day? 5) How are we all going to fit in the car? 6) You know I really like your mother, but do you think sharing a house with her for four days is such a good idea?

Now for many husbands, these concerns may seem unsettling, and could lead to either a modification of plans (you're right; let's just go to Manchester where there is lots of kosher food and it never rains); a reduction in the number of participants (we could always send a couple of the kids to friends for the weekend); or, in an extreme reaction, a cancellation of the entire idea. (Silly me, what was I thinking?!) But I am nothing if not persistent. Furthermore, I have always held a secret desire to work as a travel agent – organising trips, holidays and travel arrangements was my forte and the family knew it. There was no way I was going to let them down now, especially as the deposit for the lovely home with heated pool we were renting had already been paid – by my mother of course.

So I had it all worked out. Half of us would take the train – Hendon overland station to Brighton in 1 hour, 40 minutes – the rest of us (and Stuart, our Cavalier King Charles Spaniel) would drive down in the people carrier. As the good Jews that we are, we would first pack in all the kosher food; then, in the remaining few millimetres of space available to us, we'd contort our bodies to fit into the car. We'd organise a Tesco delivery to meet us on arrival at the house with all the other household goods we required (I even included three tubs of Ben & Jerry's Chocolate

Fudge Brownie, her favourite) and, so Tanya wouldn't have to worry about cooking, I'd make a barbeque for breakfast, lunch, supper and tea. I'd speak to my mother and make sure she'd give us enough of our own space (and I'd mention it to Dan too – it's always good to have a trusted ally in these kinds of situations.) I pointed out that it would probably be cheaper for us to actually buy the house we were renting in Brighton rather than take the whole family to Legoland for the day. And I checked the weather report; only a 30% chance of rain, which was still 47% better than London. So if you haven't realised it by now, Brian's Travel and Holiday Excursions had successfully executed the delivery of another stunning weekend break.

So there we were, strolling around the Pier, the drizzle slowly soaking through my jumper and the bulging backpack overflowing with kosher nosh, while the kids ran around spending my hard-earned cash attempting to make themselves vomit on rides that turned them upside down over the sea, or throwing large balls at smaller hoops to try and win for their youngest brother a stuffed penguin. It was at moments like this, as I recalled Tanya's reservations about the weekend, that I was confronted with an unavoidably brutal truth; my wife is much more intelligent than me.

My self-flagellation came to an abrupt end as I felt my blackberry vibrating in my pocket. Now came the tricky part, requiring both dexterity and subtlety. I needed to extract the device from my trousers pocket without Tanya noticing (I had been banned from looking at it more than fourteen times a minute), a task made even more challenging by the fact that I was pushing the pram and conversing with her at the same time. But patience is a virtue, and when she bent down momentarily to wipe some raspberry off little Mikey's face, I grabbed my opportunity. Sliding the phone surreptitiously out of my pocket with one hand, I glanced at the screen while expertly steering the pram out of the way of an oncoming ice-cream trolley with the other.

```
To; Brian Rubenstein
From; Steve Rose
Subject; Job idea
```

I began to scroll and briefly let my guard down. Mistake. Tanya made a disapproving noise and looked at me sharply. "What?' I said innocently, "This is about a job opportunity. Come on Babe, it's from Steve and could be important."

Tanya gave me one of those looks that said; "Fine, but the last tub of Chocolate Fudge Brownie is all mine," and lifting Mikey out of the pram, went in search of the maniacs – I mean children.

Left to my own devices and device, I began reading the email.

```
Hey Bri. I know you asked me to keep my
eyes and ears open for any potential
opportunities for you. Well, this is a bit
of a crazy one, but as you are unemployed
at the moment, I thought that it's at least
worth mentioning.
```

Steve was a good friend and one of the most sensitive men I knew; he ran a charity providing mental health services to the community. But at that moment, I wanted to punch him over cyberspace. Sure, I had been made redundant. But to suggest I was unemployed was going a bit far. Didn't he realise that? I mean, what was this, a challenge to see how many words in an email it took to emasculate someone? (As you can see, despite my earlier hubris, I was still working though things.)

After a few minutes, I got over myself – the truth hurts sometimes – and read on.

```
I've got this donor who owns one of the
largest car washing businesses in the
country. He's got something like 30 outlets
and it's a pretty big operation. Anyhow,
he's probably going to jail next month for
tax evasion and he's going to need somebody
to run the business for the next year or
so. I know you don't know much about car
washing and that this is coming a bit out
of left field, but as you're good with
people and strategy and all that, I thought
you might be interested. I mentioned it to
him and he thought it would a good idea to
meet you. What do you think? Let me know if
you want me to set it up?
```

I scrolled down a bit more, half expecting Steve to finish by saying he was only joking and this was just his way of letting me know he was thinking of me, but that was it - end of email. "A bit of a crazy one?" How about completely insane! I mean, I was more likely to be nominated a candidate for CEO of the Vatican than run a car washing business. I had a sudden vision of me standing in big yellow Wellies, spraying a jet hose at a luxury vehicle and conversing with a similarly outfitted colleague in an Eastern European language. It wasn't pretty.

Talk about going from the sublime to the ridiculous. This time last week I had been sitting in a credit committee meeting looking at the financial statements of a multi-million pound wind farm project in Ireland that the Bank was considering financing. Fast forward seven days and one of my close friends was trying to set up a meeting with a guy who had just been convicted of fraud and needed help running his car washing operation while he was in the slammer. As I've always said, if you're going to be religious, you've got to believe that God has a sense of humour. Steve's email was definitive proof of that; and the joke seemed to be on me.

I was about to hit delete, especially before one of my kids or an inspector from HMRC glanced at my emails, when something stopped me. To say it was a little voice on my shoulder would imply that I am either functioning on an entirely different spiritual plane or that I am psychotic. To the best of my knowledge, I am neither. What stopped me was a level of understanding that felt almost foreign. As the content of Steve's email began to sink in, a new way of thinking was threading its way into my consciousness. Suddenly I laughed out loud, startling two extensively tattooed teenagers who were walking past at just that moment. They looked at me strangely and to be fair, you couldn't really blame them; a drenched middle-aged man with an enormous backpack overflowing with children's sweets, pushing an empty pram and laughing manically at his blackberry was indeed a bit odd. Then again, we were in Brighton.

Actually, the realisation I was experiencing had occurred frequently over the last few days, not just while praying, but even when sitting at the dinner table or bathing Mikey. It had begun to transform from a willingness to let go, to move on, into something else equally intangible and difficult to describe. The best way I could explain it was a more palpable sense of the existence of Divine energy in my life.

(As I write this, a problem becomes obvious; by definition, writing about this kind of experience is nearly impossible. The world of form is described through words and images. But this is neither the language nor the dimension of the spiritual. So trying to explain what I was feeling will always fall well short. The best I can do is use the limited tools at my disposal and hope it will resonate.)

Over the years and with the help of some wonderful teachers, I've come to my own understanding of what being spiritual means. I doubt you'll find this in a Deepak Chopra book, but as I see it, it can be summed up in the following way; having a relationship with the Divine Source of everything. I've come to believe that while you can call yourself religious – as I do – that doesn't necessarily imply an active relationship with the spiritual world. What it does mean, in my opinion, is that you believe such a relationship is possible, and you're committed to trying to make that relationship work, so to speak. But to me, that's a bit similar to what it means to believe in love. A person can believe in the possibility that true, genuine love can be attained, and can seek to experience that love with another person. But that does not actually mean that you will be in love with that person. To achieve that requires shifting to another level. So too with spirituality; to be in a relationship with God requires stepping up to an entirely different plane.

While I had considered myself religious for over twenty years, for most of that time, I had been cosmetically spiritual at best. Experiencing more spirituality, actually being and feeling and living a spiritual existence, was something I found very difficult. There had been fleeting moments when I'd felt something akin to a spiritual connection, but they never seemed to last. I wanted to be more spiritual, but I also wanted to play on Centre Court at Wimbledon – some things just seemed out of reach. I had inadvertently arrived at the conclusion that while I was reasonably good at being religious, being spiritual wasn't exactly my strength. I had become stuck; willingly or not, I had settled for a kind of metaphysical mediocrity. But now it seemed as if other plans were at work – it felt like I was being offered another shot at this spirituality thing. If I could continue with the path that was opening up for me, or more accurately, was opening me up, perhaps this sense of connection I had been touching on could become embedded in my very being. It was early days yet, but I felt as though things might be starting to change.

The process of opening up had begun. Humility had started to seep back in. Perspective was being generated. The willingness to let go of things that mattered more than they should was gathering momentum. My ego was trying to land, even if it felt like it was going to be a bumpy touchdown. The effect of all of this was the emergent realisation that, in some ways, it didn't really matter what I did next from a career perspective. Of course it was relevant in terms of what my bank manager, my accountant and my father-in-law would think. But in another way, if I was going to live in integrity with the new relationship I was experiencing, if I was going to continue to open up to a different way of being in the world, it required me simply to be willing to consider just about anything that presented itself.

So rather than hitting delete, I reflected for a moment on what this email meant. It may well have been a good joke, but if I really believed that nothing is random, that everything happens for a reason, then didn't this email deserve a response? If the message here was to open up to the flow of energy in my life, I needed to start taking notice of that energy. If I was going to take a step up spiritually, I needed to take this seriously. Not because I had any aspiration to be the acting MD of a car washing business while the real boss saw out his jail sentence. But because it was my time to genuinely open up. It was time to break free from the vice-like grip of that ego for good. It was time to become more humble, so that far more could be possible. Even amidst the relative decadence of Brighton Pier, there was something that felt quite spiritual about this realisation.

I quickly typed the following reply;

```
Thanks Steve - sure I'll meet him. Let's
set it up. Thanks, Bri.
```

The day after we returned from Brighton, Ari, our sixteen year old, departed for a five day school trip to Europe. He needed to be dropped at 4am outside the school gates; suitcase, knapsack, Euros and all.

It was pitch black and pouring with rain when we pulled up behind the coach. Most of the kids had boarded already, so it was all a bit frenzied rushing Ari and his bags onto the bus amidst the constant rain bucketing down, parents bidding their children farewell and teachers attempting to oversee the whole slightly chaotic departure.

Thrusting his knapsack ahead of him, Ari put one foot on the first step of the coach, before turning to say goodbye. As he shifted his body towards me in a very teenagerly awkward attempt at a hug, I felt a strange sensation stir within me. I suddenly became highly emotional, but composed myself sufficiently to survive an uncomfortable moment. Then I leaned forward, pulling my second oldest son towards me into a brief embrace, desperate to get away before I did something highly embarrassing in front of a bus full of hyped-up students. "Have a great trip," I shouted to him in a choked-up voice above the din of the downpour, "And text us how it's going."

"Ok," Ari responded (I was grateful for getting two syllables out of him), before bounding up the coach steps and disappearing into the throng of acne-infested teenagers.

Scrambling into the car, I was relieved to be free of the incessant rain and the tumult of the impending departure. Turning the key in the ignition, I was about to pull out into the road when I burst uncontrollably into tears. The water from my eyes mixed with the showers outside so that I felt as if I was in some kind of contemporary version of Noah's Ark. And as I sat blubbering in my car, I was struck by the realisation of what was causing my emotionally unstable behaviour (which is a sensitive way of saying that I had transformed into a blabbering, blithering wreck). I was obviously deeply affected by the experience of saying goodbye to my son. But that alone didn't explain what was going on inside of me. As I drove home in the pouring rain, I was struck by the same insight that had occurred to me on Brighton Pier; I was opening up; I was starting to feel more connected – to events around me, to the possibilities of my life, to spiritual experiences, to relationships – and most poignantly, to simple everyday acts like seeing off my sixteen-year old son.

About a week later, I met with Steve's donor friend. In the end, taking on the car washing business was not the right choice – not for me and not for him. But that didn't matter. For I had learned the lesson I believed I needed to learn. By being willing, and eventually able, to open myself up to any opportunity, I was slowly becoming accustomed to a way of being that was new to me. I was learning to embrace the limitless possibilities inherent in my life, and in so doing, the sense of connection I was yearning for was beginning to feel ever more within my reach.

8. Overwhelming gratitude

Feeling gratitude and not expressing it is like wrapping a present and not giving it.
William Arthur Ward

May 29th

I had worked through the big things already; it was exactly seven days since being notified I was being made redundant, and over the past week, I had cried more than Dannii Minogue on Piers Morgan; talked things through with Tanya; broke the news to my father-in-law, mother and dog; panicked about the mortgage, pet insurance and school fees; and dusted off the CV after years of neglect. But there was one crucial conversation I kept putting off. I couldn't avoid it any longer.

For the past twenty or so years, I have woken up early every morning. Before eating, emailing or looking up the previous night's football results, I made it my priority to pray to the Master of the Universe (sorry Jose Mourinho, but that's not you). In my faith, that involves joining a quorum of at least ten men in the synagogue for a combination of prescribed communal and private prayers. On the big occasions – the birth of a child, my wedding day, the eve of the 2008 Champions League Final – I found this to be powerful and spiritually super-charged. The problem, however, lay in my own inability to make prayer a meaningful, transcendent experience on a day-to-day basis.

Sadly, early morning synagogue attendance and prayer had become my routine, somewhat akin to brushing my teeth and going to the gym. This is pretty embarrassing for an outwardly religious bloke to admit, but since I've committed to being fully truthful, there's no point in holding back now. My prayers, I'm afraid to say, had become bog standard. Truth be told, this was just not my area of expertise.

Now, standing in the synagogue in the immediate aftermath of my redundancy, I began reciting the words from the prayer book by heart, as I had done thousands of time before. And then something unusual occurred. Now I know you may be expecting the next passage to describe an extraordinary, transcendental, other-worldly experience flooding over me that would completely transform my life. Sorry to disappoint you, but that has only ever happened to me when I've been watching either Andy Murray win Wimbledon, or old re-runs of The Wire.

What happened next was an experience I had rarely known. Momentarily, I dispensed with the formal recitation of my prayer. I just stood there, my eyes closed, my head slightly bowed, and my mind quiet. I didn't meditate - at least not consciously - or think specifically about anything. I actually did nothing, and soon my soul fell silent.

And into that space came a deep feeling that I can best describe as gratitude. It was not gratitude that had an explicitly attributable source, meaning I was not grateful for this or that or anything in particular. I was simply grateful for what had happened, for what I was going through. It would be nice to say that my spiritual perspective of life facilitated my belief that everything would turn out fine, and I should just go with the flow.

That may be the case for others; it would be a fabrication for me to claim such equanimity. I didn't know where things were going, what the outcome would be or how we would pay the outstanding mortgage. But what I did know, with utter certainty, was that nothing about my life, or the events occurring within it, was random. A fundamental belief of mine is that everything which happens to us, no matter how seemingly insignificant, is meaningful and intended. While the destination may often be obscured, I am in no doubt that the journey itself is purposeful. And standing in that house of prayer, for the first time in a very long time, that sense of purposefulness became profoundly real to me. At that moment of prayer, I shifted from an intellectual experience of meaning to one that resonated with genuine feeling.

I had arrived at a deep sense of gratitude and I trusted this feeling. It came from within, not from without. In other words, it was self-generated – nobody, not my therapist, my rabbi nor even my wise wife - had told me to try and access it. Nope, this one was mine and I was going to own it. By which I mean; if this feeling was going to be of service to me in any sustainable way, I had to treat it with the respect and appreciation it deserved. (Here we go again, trying to talk about spiritual ideas with the bluntest of tools.)

So I remained in my place, fixed in private prayer, not moving nor reciting anything for a very long time. I just let the feeling wash over me. I was not trying to understand it, give it a name or attach a desired outcome. I merely absorbed it, so that when I eventually took the three customary steps backwards, signifying the end of the formal prayer, I felt an overwhelming shift within me. I hadn't consciously come to accept anything. I had just come to be.

The closest comparison I could draw to this sensation of overwhelming gratitude occurred many years previously, deep in the African bush, in a completely different time, a completely different place.

When I was eighteen, fresh out of high school, I did something pretty unusual for a white, privileged South African city kid at the time - I went to work as a safari game ranger deep in the heart of the African wilderness. Now before you think of me as some kind of African Marlboro Man, let me qualify that previous statement; I went to work as an apprentice safari ranger - the gap between apprentice and the real deal will become all too apparent in a moment.

Green as I was, in my position as apprentice ranger I was entrusted with accompanying groups of overseas tourists to a safari lodge called Mohlabetsi (don't even try pronouncing it if you're not from those parts.) It was located in a region of the country not far from the world famous Kruger National Park, where the Big Five - lion, leopard, elephant, rhino and buffalo – roam freely, and to paraphrase that classic song, the deer and the antelope play. Mohlabetsi, a small, intimate establishment, was owned and run by an old-timer, an Afrikaner by the name of Philip.

On safari, the long, stultifying afternoons are always spent in the cool shade of the main camp, protected as much as possible from the blazing heat of the African sun. But I was young, adventurous and full of pent up energy, which I was desperate to unleash on the wild habitat of Mohlabetsi. So while the guests and the animals rested up,

I, being the intrepid explorer and wannabe David Attenborough (I'm sure he was around back then already), informed Philip that I was going for a bush walk – I'd be back in time for the late afternoon safari drive with the guests. Armed with my treasured copy of *Palgrave's Guide to the Trees of Southern Africa*, I set off on my expedition.

Now, you may be asking, wasn't that a stupid thing to do? How did you know you wouldn't stumble across a dangerous animal? Why didn't you take a rifle? Did you inform Philip exactly where you were heading and how long you'd be gone? How well did you know the terrain? In the absence of obvious paths, what landmarks did you identify to make sure you could find your way back? These are perfectly reasonable questions, and in hindsight, are vital ones. However, to reiterate a point I made earlier – I was eighteen years old. That should explain it.

So off I went alone on foot into the wild bush, accompanied by my tree book and my lone brain cell. Within minutes, I had picked up the tracks of a large herd of zebra. Crouching low, imagining myself an African version of Crocodile Dundee, I began tracking the herd, eventually getting near enough to see them up close on foot. The 'hunt' was exhilarating; I lost myself in it. That wouldn't be such a serious problem if I meant I had existentially lost myself. But in this instance, what I mean is that I actually got physically lost, really lost. After some time, when I noticed the sun beginning its inexorable dip towards the horizon, I opted to return to camp; or at least I tried to return. Yet despite numerous different animal paths and directions I pursued, I could not find my way back. Somehow, I kept missing the camp. In the fast thickening shadows, every acacia tree looked the same; every termite hill a mirror image of another. I began to panic, running blindly in a desperate attempt to make it to safety before nightfall.

In the bush, on a moonless night and in the absence of any form of artificial light, when it becomes dark, it becomes very dark. Think Ten Plagues level of dark. And as blackness enveloped me in this most remote location in the heart of the African wild, surrounded by an unknown number of dangerous animals in their natural habitat, a single emotion overtook my entire being; sheer abject terror.

Unusually for a middle class urban teenager with a slight disposition towards over-reaction and hypochondria, in this instance, my panic was justified. My five senses were rendered completely redundant. (I know, not a great term to use in the context of this book's subject, but the most appropriate nonetheless.) This was an environment in which my potential adversaries were exponentially more capable of coping than I. This was their world and I was a clumsy, unwanted intruder. With none of the usual man-made resources at my disposal (the tree book didn't offer much succour), I was completely helpless. I heard sounds all around me, my imagination running amok as to who or what was responsible for them. Blinded in the pitch black, I could do nothing but await my fate – and scream.

So I did. Figuring I had nothing to lose – the animals' acute sense of hearing, smell and nocturnal vision meant they knew I was there from long before – I began screaming for Philip. As it was a small base camp, I calculated that Philip would have realised by nightfall that I had not yet returned. Although we didn't know each other too well, I was pretty sure he wasn't the sadistic, psychopathic lodge-owner type. (That characterisation was appropriate for a different guy I worked for once, and whose idea of a fun time was drunkenly shooting rounds from his double-barrelled shotgun into the thatch roof of the camp's main dining room – seriously.) So I figured Philip would be out looking for me in his Land Rover, if only to save him the bad press. Can you imagine the headline in the Game Ranger Gazette? 'Disappearance and Death in the Darkness; David Attenborough wannabe never returns from walk in the wild – tree guide book is only remains found.'

Part of me actually expected to die that night out in the bush, and I may have done so, had it not been for Philip's successful rescue mission. It was four excruciatingly long hours after darkness had fallen before the powerful spotlights atop his vehicle finally located their hapless target. The relief that flooded over my whole being as those lights came piercing through the bush towards me, was immense. As I clambered onto the back of his four wheel drive, I noticed dozens of glowing red eyes showing up in the intensely strong glare of the light. A huge herd of buffalo – enormous creatures and potentially the most dangerous in the bush - was feeding not fifty metres from where I had been standing. The noises I had been hearing weren't in my imagination at all. The danger had been very real, and very close.

As we drove back to camp, the emotions swirling within me were overwhelming. I had experienced the most intense feelings of despair, helplessness and desperation imaginable. There was not a single thing I could have done to alter my circumstances. I could only wait; my life was out of my hands.

And when the realisation fully dawned that I had been found and saved, I was overcome with the most extreme feelings of gratitude; gratitude for being alive, gratitude that for all my teenage stupidity, I was still here.

The experience of extreme gratefulness that reverberated through my prayers on the morning of May 29th brought with it a level of clarity that I don't believe I could have generated whilst at the Bank. As I had told my Mom and step-father less than a week earlier, I was beginning to understand that this job wasn't such a wonderful thing after all, that this particular version of my life was not necessarily serving me in the best possible way. The gratitude I was feeling stemmed from the sheer recognition of the 'rightness' of my redundancy. I could not, would not, have orchestrated it myself. But now that it was happening, it all seemed to be making some kind of cosmic sense.

It is impossible to overstate Tanya's role in this process. From the first moment when she heard of my redundancy, she engaged all the spiritual and psychological principles that underpin her healthy functioning. Her immediate response was; "This is absolutely what we need." She even confided in a friend that "this was perfect for our family." (Unfortunately, that friend does not work for the building society with which we have our mortgage. Still, it was a beautiful sentiment.) Tanya genuinely saw the unfolding scenario as being part of a greater plan, and so, for her, it made perfect sense to be deeply grateful for what was happening. Her conviction was infectious. Without it, I am not sure how I would have coped. With it, I was able to find the space to absorb these immensely powerful feelings of gratitude which would play such an important role in framing my spiritual and psychological response.

Of course, it's not surprising that this insight was unavailable for a long time. That's a hard lesson to learn when you're earning a decent, regular living. Such gratitude is pretty elusive when you're staying at fancy hotels, travelling business class to locations you would otherwise never visit, and drinking beer in hospitality suites at baseball games. And that's almost an impossible insight to self-generate when you wake up motivated and stimulated every morning and - assuming you've survived the tube journey - arrive at an environment that values your input and contribution. Working at the Bank had been good to me. It would take something fairly out of the ordinary for me to see it any other way.

So along comes my 'lost in the wilderness moment'. It didn't come in the form of the Big Five (I'm talking wild animals here, not consulting firms) and the sheer terror of extreme danger lurking in the pitch blackness of an African night. But it was undoubtedly accompanied by its own unique brand of fear that felt every bit as palpable.

Could I have extracted myself of my own volition? No more, I suspect, than I could have turned away from tracking those zebra almost twenty-five years ago. Now, of course, I was older and allegedly wiser; my lone brain cell at least had some friends by this stage. But that made no difference; it was just as easy to lose my bearings in my forties as it had been back then. I had gotten lost again; I could not find my way back. And so, an intervention called redundancy occurred. It was an intervention just as important as Philip's Land Rover finding me not fifty yards from a herd of buffalo. Without it, I wonder what would have become of me.

****

It's supper time. I am rarely, if ever home at this time on a weekday, but since that first meeting with Craig and Lauren over a week ago, I am no longer subject to a regular work schedule.

There is a frenetic energy at the table as the kids scramble for food. Wednesday is pasta night, so while one famished child is doling out a huge helping of noodles for himself, another is grabbing at the tomato and basil sauce Tanya has effortlessly produced, while a third is reaching over both of them to take possession of the parmesan cheese before there is none left.

"Don't use your hands," I instruct, as Sammy, our eleven year-old, heaps spaghetti onto his plate without the aid of any man-made implement. "Use the serving spoon. That's what it's there for."

Tanya throws a quick look in my direction, reprimanding me yet again that week for my tone and choice of words. I open my mouth, about to declare that they'll grow up to be savages, and no nice girls will ever want to marry them if they can't use basic implements like knives, forks and spoons, but her expression unambiguously tells me to keep quiet. The message; this isn't the time for grumpy, grouchy, bossy Dad. Just let them enjoy their supper. We'll tackle their marriage prospects another time.

I sink back into the dining room chair and fall into a reflective silence. Looking around the table, I consider each one of the young men before me.

Baruch, all seventeen years of lanky, sinewy limbs, chews noisily, shovelling copious amounts of food into his mouth. He's in a hurry – tomorrow he writes his Biology A Level, and as one of the top students in the school, he has put himself under a lot of pressure to deliver. I don't see him much these days – especially as I'm not usually around at mealtimes – but when I do, I'm profoundly struck but how much he's grown and matured. Not just vertically (he towers over me but that's not as much of an accomplishment as it sounds), but as a person. Almost without my noticing, he's absorbed so many of the values that matter to Tanya and me; personal discipline, a frightening work ethic, iron-clad integrity, self-sacrifice and spiritual commitment. He's reserved and introverted, a little self-absorbed sometimes (sound familiar?), but I'm immensely proud of him. I wish I told him that more often.

Ari is sixteen, going on twenty-six. I watch him help one of the younger ones sprinkle cheese on his pasta, and wonder how he managed to absorb all the best qualities of Tanya and myself, while jettisoning my less desirable aspects. Many say that despite his smattering of freckles and pinchable cheeks, his thick dark hair and facial features bear a close resemblance to me. The good news is that he's got a nice personality and always dresses appropriately. Like Baruch, Ari is super-smart. But he's more naturally outgoing than his older brother, making him a more likely leader. Everything seems to come easy to Ari – success in the classroom, on the football pitch, socially, wherever – but the beauty lies in the charm and humility and lightness with which he bears these gifts.

"There's no question that Froome is better than Wiggins!" Josh remonstrates with some of the fellow cycling fanatics at the table. I smile inwardly at the intensity of his views, the relentless effort to assert himself as a fourteen year-old in the midst of his noisy and opinionated siblings. He's the playful bear of the family, the one who can still be found rolling around on the floor with his younger brothers, oblivious to the demands of adolescence on his growing teenage body. His moral decision to become a vegetarian after a family holiday on a Cornwall farm three years ago is a remarkable testament to his inner kindness and sensitivity, while his capacity for enduring the endless ribbing of the two older ones is demonstrative proof of his resilience and self-belief. I clash with Josh more than any of the others at the moment (he's the one who was on the receiving end of my uncontrollable wrath back in Chapter 5), but I'm doing my best to work on it. He's got his own mind and his own rhythm. And so he should. The more I accept that, the happier he'll be.

Despite my earlier exhortations, Sammy is back scooping spaghetti out of the serving bowl with the dextrous aid of all ten fingers. Now that I've found a more contemplative space, I no longer require Tanya's guidance (that's a nice way of describing her totalitarian tendencies) in dealing with his uncouth manners. "Let him be," I tell myself. "He's a good kid and isn't going to grow up to be a terrorist, even if he occasionally behaves like one now." Sammy is the family joker – which isn't always that funny if you're his father. He's lively, loud and often ludicrous, but he's got an undeniable charm that wins him friends – and parental forgiveness – easily. His love of learning and life is infectious, as are the sparkly blue eyes that peer out amidst the ridiculously bucked teeth and rosy cheeks. He's struggling right now with the transition to secondary school, but we've seen the older boys grapple with the same challenge; he'll be fine.

He may be the slightest of the boys, but Rafi is full of energy and vim and has an adult-like maturity that belies his diminutive stature. He's only ten, yet Rafi is often the one Tanya turns to when it comes to the running of the house, imparting some instructions about meal time, or walking Stuart the dog. I listen to him inserting his opinions into the Wiggins/Froome debate, and can't help but be impressed with his bravado and self-confidence. And of course, there's his impish skill on the football pitch that often has me purring from the touchline; in spite of myself, my chest swells with pride when the father next to me turns and says; "Are you Rafi's Dad? He's quite a little player, that one."

And then, there's little Mikey, the one we waited and waited for, and the one who can bring moisture to my eyes quicker than an evicted X-Factor contestant. He sits in his high-chair taking them all in - like me; sucking his thumb - not like me; and trying to figure it all out – like me. I refuse to say I have favourites (didn't that go out with Dr. Spock or something?), but there's no question that he's got me wrapped around his little finger. Then again, everyone else in the family would probably say the same thing. He's more than just the baby brother; he's the one who keeps us all that little bit more grounded, the one who reminds us of the sheer innocence and pristine purity of life through the eyes of a small child. As I watch Tanya wipe the food from Mikey's angelic face, I cannot help but feel all the softness and gentleness and goodness within me bubbling to the surface. He's the one who, merely by flashing his gorgeous, sweet smile and his twinkling eyes, helps me find my real self when it threatens to go missing.

Sitting and observing the family having dinner, something is becoming clear to me. Without the pressures of work, which seem to always be accompanied by my own constant drive to perform, compete and prove myself, I am better able to appreciate the boys. Their zest for life and childish playfulness are more obvious; their sometimes less than perfect (although completely normal) behaviour less exasperating to me. Of course I have had periods when I've experienced this before - usually on holiday somewhere or when celebrating a religious festival or family birthday together. But as the Bank and everything associated with excelling in that environment begins to recede in my mind, I sense somehow that I may be entering a different phase where gentler, calmer feelings towards my children are more sustainable. I feel now as if I am beginning to get more in touch with that softer side of myself that I wept for so deeply only a few nights before. For the gratitude has begun to open me up, and into that space, an increased acceptance and appreciation of the unique capabilities of each one of these beautiful boys is more likely to find a home.

In between flying noodles and Tour de France predictions, Tanya catches my eye for the briefest of moments. And in that moment, all that we have created together exists as one.

As I sit and watch and listen to them all, I am overcome by the remarkable, extraordinary scene taking place around our dining room table. It's only the family having supper – just like every other night of the week – but I am forced to look away and pinch my nose, afraid the boys might see the tears that I cannot control. I have arrived at a most wonderful realisation; everything is as good as it could possibly be. For my family is before me, and in that moment, as imperfect as we all are, my life has never felt more complete, nor more blessed.

Ask anybody what the word redundancy means, and they'll respond with terms like superfluous, unnecessary and surplus to requirements. They'll tell you it conjures up feelings of being unwanted and not needed; of being a spare part at best and absolutely irrelevant at worst. And they'd be right – assuming that's what they want and expect the term to mean.

But the sense of deep gratitude that had washed over me while praying - the same feeling I experienced while sitting with the family at the dining room table on pasta night - was the beginning of a new understanding. I didn't know exactly what that meant just yet. Actually, I didn't need to know. I just needed to hold on to that feeling.

Because with gratitude comes other feelings, like abundance and fullness. It would mark the onset of a learning process for me. I had started studying again, though this time it was not for a formal qualification. I was starting to learn that redundancy could mean something entirely new and different for me.

9. The power of feeling

What lies behind us and what lies before us are tiny matters compared to what lies within us.
Oliver Wendell Holmes

May 30th
A statutory requirement of the formal redundancy process is to ensure that there are no other suitable positions available before terminating employment. That course of action had been set in motion a couple of days before the Bank Holiday Weekend, when Lauren provided me with a piece of paper listing all the roles for which they were officially recruiting.

I casually glanced at the list; a couple of roles were easy to rule out immediately;

- *Security Guard (my biceps weren't chiselled enough)*
- *IT Developer (my software skills weren't good enough)*
- *Catering Assistant (my cooking wasn't edible enough)*
- *Equity Derivatives Analyst (my brain wasn't big enough)*

But as I was about to crumple up the paper and chuck it away, one role caught my eye; Business Development Manager, Private Wealth Management. I stole another look and mulled it over. This didn't sound a million miles away from what I had been doing previously. And I knew the guys in Private Wealth pretty well; they were a good bunch with a strong leader whom I knew, liked and respected. It was worth taking a look at.

So now comes the contradiction; the paradox, the extreme irony. Here I was, one week into my redundancy, exploring all these powerful notions of gratitude, openness, humility, spirituality and the like - while at the same time, giving serious thought to applying for a role that basically amounted to helping to make rich people richer (both the clients and the bankers). To the best of my knowledge I was not experiencing any paranoid delusions, but this was bordering on schizophrenic.

The two week time period that Lauren had outlined was already rolling. But I was uncertain regarding how to proceed; I was in a kind of a no-man's land. Do I consider staying at all costs, seeking comfort in the relative security of an organisation and group of people with whom I had developed a significant attachment over the last six years? Or do I go with the feelings that had been mounting in me since that first night after being informed of Craig's decision and continue the process of building a new and different life for myself?

When I was in the Organisational Effectiveness team, I supported a chap named Tom who had been made redundant from his job in Procurement. His reaction to the notification of his redundancy astonished me at the time. Tom simply refused to accept it, claiming that the organisation was making a grave mistake. He was 54 years old and was terrified he would never find another job. So he felt he had no choice but to convince someone in the organisation to give him another chance.

My responsibility, as I saw it at the time, was to try and help him understand that his denial was unhelpful; if he could just accept the decision, he could move on and start re-building his life and career elsewhere. I pointed out that this decision had been taken after great consideration and due process, and had been authorised by a number of senior people. I observed that while his conviction that he belonged at the Bank was noble, his failure to accept reality would ultimately not serve him well. Tom listened to me respectfully but didn't change his view. Instead, he began waging an unremitting campaign to find himself another role in the company. His hope, his overwhelming belief that the situation could be turned around, was an extremely compelling force. I was concerned about Tom and convinced that his persistent denial could only lead to great disappointment, but I couldn't persuade him otherwise. I felt as though I was standing idly by, watching someone hang themselves.

But then a crazy thing happened. Tom landed a job in IT. His redundancy was rendered null and void. To his immense credit, he had refused to accept both the situation and the final decision. Sure, he had to change roles. But he managed to stay at the Bank, remaining part of an organisation where he felt he belonged and where he could continue to earn a decent living. I was delighted to be proven wrong and was genuinely happy for him.

It dawned on me that I had arrived at the exact same cross-roads as Tom. The two week consultation period afforded me the selfsame possibility that Tom had clung onto so tenaciously; to look for another role within the organisation, not to let go until I found something that would render the redundancy process, if you'll excuse the pun, redundant. Yet still, the questions continued to swirl around my cluttered mind; did I accept the proposed redundancy, or should I try and find a way around it? Did I fight or flight? Did I listen to my own advice from a couple of years previously and not allow myself to be seduced by hope? Or should Tom's story serve as my inspiration for going out and finding another position within the Bank? I remained unsure and unable to decide, waiting instead to see what would transpire before committing myself either way.

Well, the truth, as I discovered in Tom's case, is that hope is a very powerful thing. So I rationalised pursuing the Private Wealth opportunity, insisting to Tanya, myself and anyone else who would listen, that; 1) it didn't make sense to just walk out of a good organisation after six productive years without first exploring all possible options; 2) I could always take this role and at the same time look for something else outside of the Bank; and 3) we needed the money. All of these (especially #3) were highly compelling reasons, even though they seemed to miss the point of my new-found insights regarding striving for greater softness, meaning, and all that New Age stuff.

The simple reality was that it was hard to leave, especially as it was not of my own volition. While I was extremely ambivalent about the potential new role, I told myself that much better to go when I wanted to rather than when they told me to go - master of your own destiny and all those good ideas. My rationalisation went so far as to convince myself that if I was actually offered the role, I could always say no, which would in turn allow me to feel much better about this whole sordid affair. I mean it; I really thought that one up.

The first step was an initial meeting with Brett who ran that part of the business. Brett and I were reasonably friendly outside of work, which is unusual for me (having non-canine friends I mean). I knew him as a very straight-forward guy who would be direct, honest and fair. The fact that we were friends would only become a factor if our wives got involved, meaning that his wife would probably push for me to get the job while Tanya, who had already starting dreaming of a more serene life for us independent of the Bank, would call him late at night, assume a deep voice, breathe too loudly into the telephone like in one of those old horror films, and gravely intone; "I know what he did last night. He's not for you. Don't give him the job or you'll never see your children again."

Brett had his own reservations – I never found out if Tanya's Nightmare on Elm Street impersonation influenced him regarding the correct next step for me and the firm. He mentioned he knew many people who had been uncertain about leaving the Bank, but once they had taken that decision, or had it made for them, they invariably landed on their feet. "I can't think of one person who isn't better off since they left," Brett stated emphatically. But in spite of his sage remarks, I wasn't really able – or willing - to hear them. Leaving was still incredibly difficult to contemplate as long as there was another internal option to consider. I was living on hope, and as I had discovered, hope is a powerful drug.

So I convinced Brett and myself that I was up for this. "It's true that I don't have much of a track record in terms of bringing in High Net Worth individuals. (That's banking speak for really, really, really rich people.) But I know quite a lot of reasonably well-off people and I've got a pretty good list of wealthy folk on my blackberry, which is a decent place to start," I proposed to Brett. "I even know someone who knows the dog-walker of Cheryl Cole's ex-mother-in-law's hairdresser. I'm sure I could get us a meeting with her." (I meant Cheryl, not the dog-walker.)

Brett looked at me sceptically, knowing that as an ardent Man U fan, I was very unlikely to have even the most tenuous link to the ex-wife of a former Arsenal player. So shifting gears to include a strategic rationale for how I could support the Private Wealth business, I persisted; "Don't forget I've been around this place for nearly six years. I know almost all the people and teams down on the first floor." I was just getting going now as I went into corporate-speak overdrive. "There are enormous potential synergies to build out our value proposition and data we could be generating from mining our Customer Relationship Management system, not to mention the multiple revenue opportunities to be exploited if we took a more holistic view of each client and transaction, and the leverage we should be extracting through the corporate and institutional channels as well as the investment banking platform, assuming high levels of collaboration and internal networking."

I was slightly out of breath but sat back smugly, pleased with myself and my multi-syllable words. Brett, a successful and no-nonsense business leader, looked at me as if Iran had just denounced its nuclear proliferation programme. Still, he must have been impressed with something I'd said - or maybe he just wanted to shut me up – because he suggested that I meet with the various Private Wealth team heads over the next couple of days and take it from there.

"So what did Brett say?" asked Tanya as soon as I reached her on the phone. I heard a noise in the background that strongly resembled one son throwing another son down the stairs but chose to ignore it. Staying focussed is very important for a successful career.

"He was positive," I replied, trying to play it cool.

"Ah, that's a pity," Tanya said. "I was so hoping he'd tell you it was a no-go."

She really is a supportive wife; you've just got to get to know her.

"Well, sorry to disappoint you Sweetie. But he thinks it's worth chatting to the other guys running the various teams up there. So let's wait and see what happens, but I'm hopeful it may actually turn into something."

I was going to say something else but then I heard another noise that sounded oddly like one son banging another son's head against a wall. "Gotta go," I said quickly, "speak later." As I said; focus is key.

The next couple of days were a whirlwind of internal interviews and meetings. As I developed a better idea of the strategic direction of the business, it started to sound pretty good. The Bank clearly wanted to develop this part of its franchise - there were clients to be found, relationships to be developed and a solid business opportunity to be explored. Yet a nagging feeling kept gnawing away at me. Try as I might, I was finding it really hard to get excited about this role. I knew Tanya felt ambivalent about it (that's a politically correct way of saying that she thought it was a terrible idea). But as I'm a grown man who makes his own decisions every now and again, I realised I must clarify for myself whether this job was right for me, assuming they offered it. I needed to determine not whether this was a job I could do, but whether this was a job I should do. So seeking constructive advice, I sought out Aaron, a good friend of ours who always has a unique perspective on things.

We met at a funky coffee shop of his choosing in Clerkenwell. He only eats fresh food (how weird is that?) and I only eat kosher (how normal is that?) so it was just cappuccinos for us both. After commenting on how good he looked – what else do you say to a guy whose idea of letting his hair down from a culinary perspective is to add a handful of raw cashews to his nut and raisin mix – I outlined my dilemma. I explained the pros and cons of the proposed role, analysing the opportunity in detail and assessing its veracity. My uncertainty was based on questioning whether I was merely playing it safe by taking a role that though it didn't really grab me, would offer a good income, develop some new skills and ensure that I remained part of the firm. On the other hand, I stressed that at the age of 42, I had arrived at a point in my life where I was reluctant to make a decision that felt somewhat expedient. I talked about how this decision felt almost existential in nature – it was more than being about just taking a good job – but I doubted whether I had the courage to back up that way of thinking. In general, I was doing what I did best – or at least what I knew how to do best. I was thinking it through a lot, attempting to apply my intellect to tackle what appeared to be a complex predicament. Only problem was that it wasn't getting me anywhere.

Aaron listened quietly, as he always does, and then floored me with the following;

"Well, it seems to me Brian that you're trying to make a deep, spiritual decision from your analytical mind. Now the problem with that is that it's the wrong tool. The analytical mind can't access that deeper, more profound space. So you're trying to think up the solution, when really you should be asking yourself; 'does it feel right?' You won't solve this one satisfactorily with the analytical mind, so try switching it off and get in touch with what you feel."

I almost expected Aaron, one of the smartest, most grounded people I know, to jump up and start singing that old campfire classic, Kumbaya. Fortunately, we were in a public place. And I don't think he likes singing. Switch off my analytical mind? What was he talking about? I mean, come on - surely that's my biggest asset? (People also tell me that I have very nice eyebrows but I don't think it's appropriate to mention here.) How else was I going to have a chance at making a sensible decision?

But as often happens with me when I bother to stop talking and start listening, something seeped in. So before telling him he was completely nuts (which wasn't far from the truth as that's just about all he eats) and calling for the bill, I let his comments sink in a little. While Aaron waited patiently for me to digest what he was saying, my mind flashed to another critical decision that Tanya and I needed to confront a couple of years ago.

As you may have already worked out, we have quite a lot of children; six sons to be precise. But before you accuse us of being highly irresponsible, disdainful of global food shortages or just completely out of sync with the national average of 1.7 children per family, bear in mind that many of our friends also have large families. Indeed, having a family of this size is quite the norm in the community in which we live. As a matter of fact, our neighbours have ten kids, so in a way we aren't even keeping up with the Joneses – or the Cohens in this instance.

Tanya had always wanted to have a large family, so the first five came thick and fast. By the time I was 32 and Tanya a mere 29, we were already bursting at the seams in our 2 ½ bedroom house in Hendon. To illustrate; Rafi, our youngest at the time, was sleeping in a travel cot in the laundry cupboard. I'm serious. Harry Potter's first abode under the stairs was luxurious in comparison. The time had come to build on – our 10th anniversary gift to ourselves was a loft extension, giving us two more bedrooms on the third floor. For most normal families this would be a comfortable fit of seven in a home – two sharing one of the larger bedrooms and the rest with enough of their own space. (Actually, I was also sharing a bedroom – with Tanya fortunately.)

But as we have often struggled with being classified as a normal family, we were not afraid to tackle the status quo. Thus, we began asking ourselves whether the proportion of children to rooms should be subject to a strategic review. From a resourcing perspective, (as you can see, I still haven't quite lost my capacity for corporate-speak,) we needed to assess the long term sustainability of having only a single gender family - even Stuart the dog is a male. In a nutshell, we were asking ourselves the following; should we have more children? Specifically, should we try for a girl - one more time?

So we spent a serious amount of time grappling with this dilemma. There were so many considerations, some of which were more spiritual in nature, some more practical. A sampling; we've got a wonderful family; isn't it perfect the way it is? How will eight of us fit into a seven seat people carrier? It would be so nice for the kids to have a baby brother or sister. We've already got a decent five-a-side team; why do we need a sub (unless she's a cheerleader)? Tanya is doing so well in her career and helping so many people; how will having another child affect all of that? Have you seen our overdraft – how will we cope with one more? Wouldn't it be special to bring another soul into the world?

Tanya and I discussed the matter at length, throwing around these and so many other questions and possible answers as we sought clarity on such a crucial issue. Though both of us were desperate for a little girl, we came to realise that this decision needed to be based on whether we thought our family was complete as it was. Statistics (damned statistics) indicated we were likely to have another boy anyway, so by virtue of the odds, the gender issue receded into the background. Having a large family was an important value of ours, rooted in our faith and belief system. But having another child, after an eight year gap, was a difficult commitment to make. Certainly, a part of us was convinced we had already passed this stage in our lives. We were confused. Try as we might, we could not arrive at a resolution. We asked the opinion of others' whose advice we valued; we carefully considered every angle; we even consulted a psychic. (Just kidding, but Tanya did genuinely try and convince me of it. A man has got to draw the line somewhere.) We waited; and we waited some more.

But still the clarity did not come. No matter how much we applied our minds, no matter how hard we thought about it, we just could not figure out the right thing to do. And then it dawned on us (or more accurately, it dawned on Tanya, but as I'm an equal partner in this co-creation thing, I'm going to take some credit where it's not due). Our problem wasn't that we were not thinking clearly or hard enough. It lay, paradoxical as it may sound, in thinking too much. We were trying to think our way through an intensely personal, deeply spiritual issue. And as we belatedly came to realise that we were getting nowhere, we stopped thinking and allowed ourselves to feel. Suspending our overactive mental activity, we instead tried to get in touch with our deep, inner feelings, asking ourselves a fundamental question; what really felt right?

Not surprisingly, before long, the answer became absolutely clear. Boy or girl, we wanted another child. It was right for us and our family. How did we know? Because it felt right; simple as that. (Three years on from arriving at that conclusion, we are blessed with a beautiful little boy who has just celebrated his second birthday. It is impossible for Tanya or me, or any of his adoring brothers, to fathom any other reality than having precious little Mikey in our lives. I shudder to imagine what might have happened had we given our rational thinking just a little more credibility.)

By the time I had finished with these ruminations in that vibey little coffee shop, Aaron's coffee had ice cubes hanging from it. Sometimes I can be a little slow (not when I'm running mind you), but now it had become clear to me; Aaron was absolutely right. I wasn't going to solve this one by thinking it through. I had already tried that and it hadn't worked. So how was thinking about it some more going to help? Would I become significantly more intelligent in the next ten minutes? Would I find a new pro or a different con to the ones I had already spent the last couple of days considering? Nope, this was indeed about a feeling.

And in that moment, I had my answer. It didn't feel right. The Private Wealth role wasn't the right role for me. I didn't need hope – it was the wrong drug for me.

As that realisation dawned, I glanced at Aaron, who was grinning at me rather strangely. I looked around frantically, desperately searching for a guitar and a campfire. The words 'Kumbaya my Lord' were ready to roll off my tongue.

The next day, Friday, I met with Brett to hear his verdict following my meetings with his various business heads earlier in the week. I was reluctant to tell him that I had serious reservations about taking the position. I thought that would be disingenuous considering I had put myself forward for the role in the first place. Instead I wanted to hear where they stood.

Brett did his best to be gentle; "We don't think it's going to be quite the right fit Brian. I'm sorry."

I smiled and then surprised him. "I agree absolutely Brett; it's not right for me. It would be like trying to fit a square peg into a round hole. So thanks for that – I actually feel pretty relieved that you didn't offer me the role. It just didn't feel right to me either."

Brett looked slightly perplexed but I think he got it. I had given due respect to the power of feeling; there was nothing left to discuss.

The two weeks were now up - I had explored the final option at the Bank, and it hadn't panned out. It was time to leave – for good.

III

Understanding

If there is no spirituality, there is no true wisdom.
The beginning of all wisdom is being in awe of God.
The Talmud

10. What's holding me back?

If we focus our attention on techniques, on specific practises, on to do lists...we might make some small improvements. But if we want to move ahead in a major way, we need to shift our paradigm and see the situation in a totally new way.
Steven Covey

June 3rd

People have different ways of organising themselves mentally. Some keep a diary. Others follow particular routines that make sense to them. The old school investment banker types rely on their PA's. Me, I write lists; long, copious lists. It used to be on scraps of paper or in small notebooks I could fold into my suit pocket. But as befitting the modern man I've become, I now type my lists into my Blackberry. If I was to lose that little electronic device, I would be really stuck. Not only because I wouldn't know whom to email, phone or text, but also because I wouldn't be able to remember which son I am taking to football practice next Tuesday night. My daily 'to do' list sometimes resembles the length of a Tolstoy novel. My 'to email' list is often almost as long. My 'ideas to follow up on' list could make me either really famous one day, or become highly embarrassing should it ever fall into the wrong hands. You get the picture; I am a list man through and through. Without my lists, I feel lost, uncertain and – you'll have to forgive me for this one – listless.

Not surprisingly, now that the two week redundancy process was over and my new situation official, I began writing, or more accurately, typing several lists. My first list was entitled 'What to do next';

```
1. Speak to mortgage company
2. Find an employment lawyer
3. See if I can get the money back for my
pre-paid personal training sessions
4. Update CV
5. Start job search
6. Cancel the romantic 20ᵗʰ Anniversary
holiday to Mauritius (we hadn't actually
booked anything yet but a man can dream,
can't he?)
7. Arrange therapy sessions
```

Another list was called; 'Internet Searches';

```
1.Books on redundancy (a limited selection;
hence this lengthy discourse)
2.Redundancy support groups
'Make Redundancy the best thing that ever
happened to you. Join now for just £9.99 a
month.' You've got to be kidding.)
3.Cheap family holidays in the greater
Slough region.
4.Easy ways to get a book published.
5.Ex-banker success stories.
```

And still a further, more significant, list was titled; 'Who to contact'. This was undoubtedly my longest list – I wasn't sure if my Blackberry had enough memory to absorb all the names I typed in. I started by going through my entire sequence of contacts, applying the criteria that no matter how remote the possibility, anybody who could possibly assist me in any way should be included on the list. The result was an eclectic mix of names that required some editing; I ended up having to delete Mrs. Goldberg (my Year 8 History teacher), the cranial osteopath, our plumber, and my personal trainer – there was no way he was going to give me my money back.

Even after this culling process, the list remained exceptionally long. On the one hand, I was encouraged – I had a lot of people to whom I could reach out for help. On the other hand, I was also a little overwhelmed; where should I start?

Being the brilliantly creative individual that I am, I rigorously applied my mind to this dilemma, concluding that the best place to begin was with the letter 'A'. So skipping the AA Emergency Response Team (I hadn't had a breakdown - yet), Aaron – my Kumbaya fresh food eating friend from the trendy coffee shop - came first. And so I got stuck into it, phoning, emailing and texting everyone and anyone who had made my list, reaching out and seeking assistance, support and guidance.

Not everyone replied, but overall, the response from friends, family, colleagues and the entire cast of Les Miserables was overwhelming. Most people were simply happy to help as best they could; I was deeply touched by their concern and generosity of spirit.

Of course, not every call or email was easy to make or send; I needed to get over myself to contact a former colleague at the Bank with whom I had some unresolved issues (I must have told him a million times it was my stapler.) There were others I just hadn't spoken to in so long that it felt awkward to re-initiate contact under these trying circumstances. In one such instance, a former senior person at the Bank offered some blunt feedback, chastising me for not having reached out to him when he left the organisation and only making contact now when I was seeking his help. He was right of course, and I apologised contritely. We ended up having a very good conversation; his considered input was extremely helpful in the initial few days of my redundancy.

So I continued to work through my list in a whirlwind of frenetic activity, as I set up meetings, fired off emails and generally put myself about. What resulted were some fascinating discussions that led me in all kinds of unexpected directions, both mentally and practically. No further car washing opportunities came my way, but a whole lot of other unusual ideas began to emerge.

Near the top of my list was Jack, whom I met for breakfast at Brent Cross shopping centre one morning soon after I received the redundancy news. I first got to know Jack when he was guest-lecturing on my MBA course, and I am proud to consider him a mentor ever since. He is my opposite in so many ways; a committed Christian to my Jewish orthodoxy; rural and working class Scottish by birth and breeding to my relatively privileged suburban Canadian-South African upbringing; father of two older daughters in their thirties to my Boys' club. Jack had lived a fascinating life, having started his working career as a sixteen year-old boy in the mines of Scotland almost a half century ago. Although we come from such radically diverse experiences and backgrounds, Jack and I (as well as his wife Isabel and Tanya) share a bond and understanding that is very special.

As we began talking, Jack was his usual self; wise, caring, insightful and always open to considering situations in a different light. Still, he definitely caught me off-guard when he asked between mouthfuls of scrambled egg whether I would be interested in managing hospitals. Jack always thought of things a bit differently – his work on *Attractive Leadership* includes some of the most creative ideas I have come across – but this felt like it really came out of left field.

"Why would you suggest that?" I asked him.

"I don't know exactly", Jack replied, "the idea just kind of came to me while I was driving down the A406 to come and meet you. The people who do a bad job of it usually end up in notoriety on the front page of the newspaper. But the people who are really good absolutely love it and make the most fantastic contribution. So I thought that with your transferable skills, it might be something for you to consider."

I loved it. Not necessarily the specific idea of managing a hospital – I didn't have the slightest clue what that entailed – but the thought that I was now completely free even to contemplate such ideas. Suddenly I felt liberated; I could begin exploring new horizons and new ways of thinking about myself. So I contacted another good friend in our community who is one of the country's foremost neurosurgeons. Dr. Jeffrey promptly put me in touch with the Chief Executive of a large private hospital who graciously made the time to meet and share with me what such a role involved. This story doesn't necessarily have a fairy-tale ending. I am not currently writing this from a plush executive office on the third floor of a medical facility, now under my management. But that's not the point. Rather, as Aaron had taught me, if an idea felt right, it was worth investigating further to see what might emerge. And who knows where the energy and flow of things might lead? As George, another wise guide said to me; as long as you're open to it, the right opportunity will find you.

The acts of kindness and support were often relatively small, but nevertheless they still carried significant meaning. Anthony, an old friend and busy Chief Operating Officer of a fast-growing hedge fund, insisted on picking me up from the tube station. We had a great chat in the local park. Richard, a highly successful analyst at Goldman Sachs, who attended the same school as I in Johannesburg thirty years ago, called and emailed regularly, offering help and support at every turn. There was a former employer who wisely articulated the unique contribution he thought I could make to the local community, and in so doing, made a significant impact on my thinking. Grant, Global Head of Sales at one of the world's best-known car manufacturers, and the husband of an old school friend, met up with me for a beer one night. When I suggested sending him my CV to forward to a few people, his emphatic response was a big boost to my confidence; "I don't need to see your CV Brian. I think you're smart, but more importantly, you're honest, really honest, and that's reason enough for me to recommend you if I hear of anything."

Pete, founder and director of his own extremely successful Legal Search company, texted me after 11pm one night asking if it was too late to call. I responded by saying that it wasn't too late but that I felt bad keeping him up at this time of night – we could speak the next day.

Don't want to miss the chance to give an old friend some advice, he texted back immediately. Will call in five minutes. P.

In those final days, as I packed up and said goodbye at the Bank, many colleagues expressed their dismay at my departure in unusual but caring ways. James, head of the Equity Capital Markets team, found me next to the copying machine; "I was shocked to hear you're leaving," he proclaimed, looking genuinely upset and perplexed.

"Why?" I asked him.

"Because I really liked you," he replied.

"Thanks." I was touched by his kind words, though somewhat puzzled by the relevance of his comment.

Still, his and other such sentiments meant a lot. Colleagues were genuinely surprised and saddened to see me go. The reaction of Earl, the big, burly security guard from Nigeria who supported Liverpool but nonetheless greeted me effusively every morning as I came through the front entrance, epitomised the reaction of many; "Noooooooooooooo", he exclaimed when I informed him of my news. "I'm so sorry to hear that. How can it be?"

I was briefly tempted to ask Earl to raise the issue with Craig Hertford, armed with his Taser stun gun, but desisted.

Meanwhile, my good friend Jimmy appeared bereft at my impending departure. I had been at the Bank a while already when Jimmy arrived to join our Internal Audit team and he often used me as a sounding board for advice regarding his own personal and career decisions. We worked on the same floor and made a point to try and connect daily, either over lunch, coffee, an unsuccessful shopping spree to NEXT or an upper body work-out at the gym. Jim and I had grown close over the last few years; he was my best friend and confidant at work.

"So, what you gonna do next Bri?" Jimmy asked while spotting me on the bench press. We were at the gym, the day before I was officially due to leave.

I grunted something unintelligible in response; I was really struggling on my seventh rep at 75kgs - this wasn't the best time to have this conversation.

Jimmy seemed unperturbed. He was used to my grunting by now, especially when I couldn't fit into the Extra Slim-Fit shirts at NEXT, and continued with the discussion while seemingly oblivious to the bar wavering dangerously above my chest. "You'll be fine I'm sure. You've got a lot of experience and a nice collection of ties – something will turn up." (Somebody's always got to be the funny guy.)

Then he paused and grew serious for a moment. "But man, I'm gonna miss you."

I would have liked to thank him for his support, emotional resonance and bad sense of humour, but at that very moment, I had 75 kilos of iron trapped on my torso – I had failed on my ninth rep.

"Jim," I managed to hiss as the breath slowly squeezed from my lungs. "Get this thing off of me first – we'll have a hug later!"

That night, I received a long email from Jimmy. While lying prostrate on the couch, pressing a bag of frozen peas against my aching pectoral muscles, I read his mail.

```
Subject; The Best Friend I Ever Did Have

I didn't quite finish what I wanted to say
earlier, so here goes.
I suppose this is a good time to write. To
write about all the ways you've impacted
me. You've been more than a friend. You've
listened when times were hard and made them
somewhat easier. You listened when my
thoughts were blurred and made them
```

```
clearer. You never judged me, never lost
patience with me.
I'm not sad because you've moved on, that's
the way of the world. No. Rather I'm sad
because part of me has moved on. I've often
thought the reason I moved to this company
was to meet you. Maybe you simply needed to
have an impact on my life and then move on.
Remember the coffee talks, the walks, the
football matches, the single run by the
Thames, the countless visits to the bank,
the aborted trips to NEXT.
You taught me what friendship meant and I'm
so grateful for all the wisdom you shared
with me. Be sure to share your wisdom with
others. Write, talk, teach, share, consult,
fix, repair and then some more. You and
your wife are a blessing to all who know
you.
Forever grateful ... drastically improved,
Jimmy
```

Of all the messages I received after being informed of my redundancy, this one touched me the most deeply. I was so moved by Jimmy's words that I almost expected a celestial angel to appear at any moment, playing a harp while the stars above aligned themselves. It's a good thing we were both happily married.

There were many other messages of support, and numerous friends and colleagues who stepped forward to help, each of whom lent their own personal brand of encouragement, wisdom and kindness. Some of these emails, meetings and conversations achieved little in terms of progressing my job search in a practical sense. Some helped to crystallise my thinking; others led to further meetings with their contacts. And some had no discernible benefit at all. But without exception, everyone made a contribution to my well-being. They showed they cared and this, more than anything else, mattered to me. I realised how blessed I was to share a connection with so many special people, who in one form or another, were willing to help as best they could.

June 6th

One of the key people on my 'seek advice list' was Rabbi Dr. David Katz, once a leading physician in Canada, now a well known author and speaker on Jewish philosophy and medical ethics. I had known him longer than I knew Tanya – we went back almost twenty-five years. In the early days of exploring my faith and its meaning for me, he had been an immense source of inspiration with his constant guidance, teachings and personal care. I was not unusual in that regard; thousands of people throughout the world (he has lectured everywhere from Johannesburg to Jerusalem; Sydney to St. Louis) have benefitted from his unique combination of spiritual wisdom, deep humility and intellectual and personal integrity. He is now a man in his sixties, a father and grandfather many times over, but he has never lost his incredible energy and capacity to contribute.

There is however one issue between us that has never been resolved. As a rabbi, doctor and man of immense integrity, I thought it would be completely safe to share one of my deepest, darkest secrets with him – that Tanya was a faster runner than I. Now this was a hard thing for me to do. But I needed someone to confide in – a man of faith who would guide me out of my desolation and despair every time Tanya accelerated up an incline.

But rather than providing me with the kind of support you would expect from a spiritual teacher – compassion, empathy, a metaphysical perspective perhaps – he reacted to this deeply personal confession in a way that I found highly disconcerting. He laughed; I mean really laughed. He thought it was the most hysterical thing he'd ever heard. And every time we saw each other thereafter, with his mischievous wink and a little nudge to the ribs, Rabbi Katz reminded me of the Lord's inequitable distribution of natural running talent between husband and wife. He thought the matter so funny that, when I invited him to address my oldest son at his Bar Mitzvah celebration, he chose to open with his version of a joke; the one about the host whose wife was faster than he. Unbelievably, he actually shared this with a room full of a hundred guests. Though most of them were close family and friends, I was devastated. I didn't go out in public for a month.

As I said before, I need to get over myself.

It was the beginning of the third week post redundancy, and we were seated at a table at Rabbi Katz's favourite over-priced kosher restaurant on Golders Green High Street. I was going through one of my low-carb phases so poked around at my salad nicoise unenthusiastically while the rabbi/doctor tucked into his toasted cheese bagel. Diminutive in size but enormous in stature, the Rabbi fixed me a look with his penetrating blue eyes while he stroked his grey beard. I'd just given him the detailed low-down of my situation. His response was succinct and unambiguous.

"I've watched you for a long time from the side, Brian. And it was not my place to interfere, especially when you seemed to be doing well at your job. But you're a person who could really leave his mark, in my opinion. So here's the key question for you; what's holding you back?"

Sometimes people ask you something that doesn't add much value to your life. What's the fastest land mammal? Who is better – Messi or Ronaldo? Why did it never work out between Jennifer and Brad? (This one has always bothered me). And then, sometimes, a question gets asked of you that is so big, so meaningful to your life, that it kind of stops you in your tracks. This was one of those types of questions. Rabbi Katz – supplier of wisdom and perspective to me for over a quarter of a century had done what he always did so well – got right to the heart of it. I looked back at him across the table, my mind blank.

And then the insight hit me like a ton of bricks. I wasn't being held back by anyone, or anything. I was being held back by me; I was doing this to myself, one hundred per cent unaided. While I didn't know exactly what I was doing that was holding me back, I instinctively knew that figuring out the answer to that question would be absolutely crucial in terms of determining what would come next in my life.

This wasn't about a list, about what to do or who to contact. This wasn't about making some small changes, or executing an existing strategy, or revisiting something that hadn't quite worked in the past. This question was about something far more fundamental, something that required an enormous shift in my thinking, something that would bring me to a level of understanding that seemed, until this moment, to be inaccessible to me.

Over the past couple of weeks, my life had changed irrevocably. Being made redundant had shattered my illusions, the self-image under which I had been labouring for so long. Leaving the Bank, having the opportunity to reflect on what I had learned from this experience, had helped me access a degree of humility; it gave rise to a perspective which allowed me to perceive myself and my career in a completely new light. But there was still something missing – and the answer to that potentially life-changing question of 'what's holding me back' was at the heart of that something. With that answer would come understanding – real, deep, self-understanding. I would have to find that answer. My journey demanded it.

11. Regular Guy

A man should never be ashamed to own he has been in the wrong, which is by saying, in other words, that he is wiser today than he was yesterday.
Alexander Pope

July 3rd

It's been almost five weeks since I left the Bank. The month of May, with all its melodrama and life-changing consequences, seems so long ago. It's been a busy time, almost manic. Tanya complains she is seeing less of me than when I worked in the City. It's true. I've been following up on my 'What to do next' list and 'Who to contact list', and a zillion other lists with feverish intensity. Countless meetings, calls, emails have been fired off daily. I've been totally immersed in the process of trying to figure out the next step for me and my career. I've been working hard, pedalling fast, but the bicycle doesn't feel like it's going anywhere.

Now though, I have stopped. The first light of day is just emerging as I stand on the balcony of a gorgeous little place I am renting for a few days called 'The Boathouse'. It offers the most serene view over the Swinomish Channel, the gentle river which runs through the picturesque historic town of La Conner, Washington State, on the north-western tip of the United States. My knowledge of American geography is pretty much limited to my experience of a couple of big cities on the Eastern Seaboard, but if there is a more charming, peaceful town to be found in this enormous melting pot of a country, I find it hard to believe. The branches of the towering pine trees sway ever so slightly in the gentlest of breezes. A flock of majestic geese fly gracefully past, low over the water, their outstretched wings skimming the surface. The river shimmers in the early morning light. The colour of the pre-dawn sky is an exquisite blend of pink, blue and gray. The mist cloaks the looming peaks of Mt. Vernon like a veil enveloping a waiting bride. There is nothing to hear but silence. I am deeply quiet; profoundly moved. The world is perfect and I feel so privileged to be in it.

It is no surprise that I am praying again. The mystical sources of my tradition explain that the most powerful spiritual time of the day is sunrise - that exact moment when night meets day, when the brilliant life-giving force of the golden orb breaches the horizon. I am rarely awake at this time, but extreme jetlag has had me up for a while, and for once, I have no excuse for not making the most of such a precious moment. The time and place are almost as perfect as can be in the world of the finite.

The tears come hard and fast again – I can't control them as my body shudders under their effect. But these tears are different from those shed previously. There is no obvious sadness now; no pain or hurt. I am unfamiliar with these kinds of tears, but somehow I sense they are ones to embrace. There is a cathartic feeling to them; they have a humbling, opening, connecting quality. I welcome the outpouring with deep gratitude, for however clichéd this may sound, they feel like tears of the soul. And that can only be a good thing.

I have just returned from an invigorating pre-dawn run across the river and through the local Indian reservation, which got me to thinking about something taught to me by my good friend Bobby, who introduced me to marathon running way back. A veteran of countless ultra-long distance races, Bobby ain't the quickest guy around, but he's surely one of the most dogged. Yet despite usually deferring to his far greater experience, I was taken aback on one of our early training runs together when he did something which seemed bizarre at the time – he walked. Now there's nothing wrong with walking; unless you're meant to be running. But in Bobby's case, when he got tired or just needed to change strategy, either mentally or physically, he would walk for a while. Admittedly, that is not an advisable approach if you're intent on winning an Olympic medal or even coming in at sub-three hours (or in my case, sub-four). But as the vast majority of marathon runners will finish somewhere between four and five-and-a-half hours, it means that they will walk at some stage, if not many stages, of the race. And Bobby showed me that not only was that acceptable; it was actually a pretty good idea. Because to run 26 miles without breaking up the pace with short stretches of walking, is an incredibly difficult thing for most of us. So the odd walk, mixed in with a predominance of running, is the most likely way to make it to the finish line.

But walking during a marathon requires a dose of humility. It requires being able to take a step back, to generate sufficient perspective to say to yourself; "I'm probably not going to win this thing. Actually, I may not even finish in the time I'm aiming for. But that's cool, because the real aim is to finish. That's the achievement; getting to the finish line – in my own time, in my own way."

Naturally there have been occasions when the sheer exhaustion that ensues from running considerably long distances has forced me to walk. But I've always viewed this as a moment of weakness; of letting myself down. Yet, when I have actually made it to the finish line, the sense of self-achievement is so immense, so deep an expression of pushing myself beyond my normal levels, that it becomes clear how a bit of walking, now and again, simply does not matter. I've come to recognise that if I'm willing to find sufficient humility, there is a very profound lesson to be learned; that it's okay to walk.

Reframing my running strategy in this manner made good sense. Yet when it came to applying the same insights to rebuilding my career, they eluded me. My initial feelings of gratitude, openness and humility were at odds with an overwhelming compulsion to keep running – to go from this job to the next. This manic-type state made it almost impossible for me to consider that I might need to slow down, to walk a little in-between. I had typically managed the events of my life quite dextrously and at breakneck speed, but now, such power was no longer in my hands. It occurred to me that I was desperately struggling with the sense of a loss of control; I couldn't engineer what was happening to me in any way, nor accelerate its change. This compounded the sense of failure, frustration and inadequacy. At the same time, I couldn't let go, and step off the treadmill, even for a brief while. I felt trapped.

By the time I settled into my seat on the North American-bound flight, I was exhausted, both mentally and physically. As I ran around manically trying to find the right opportunity, I found myself becoming emotionally overwrought. Writing and re-writing my CV; emailing and calling friends, contacts and acquaintances; setting up meetings and then attending them with the requisite focus and energy – all were becoming increasingly difficult. I felt adrift and demoralised. I'm not prone to depression, but this felt pretty close. Despite – or perhaps because of - all the frantic activity, I couldn't seem to muster the psychological strength to alter my mindset. I was setting a frenetic pace and struggling to keep up.

I was pretty certain, together with Tanya's constant reassurance, that I would land a job; I had already received a couple of half-offers and some consulting opportunities. Sure, I wasn't going to receive a City-like salary, but I was fine with that. I had already decided I didn't want to return to that world, and we were both willing to make the necessary sacrifices and adjustments. Still, I was desperate to find the 'right job' – one that would offer fulfilment and purpose, in addition to bringing out the best of my composite experience and skills. I was driving myself relentlessly in the quest to obtain a new position, but it wasn't materialising, and I was becoming increasingly tormented by the wait. And the longer it took, the more frustrated I became.

At the end of one long, emotionally draining day of following up potential opportunities that didn't seem to be leading anywhere, Tanya laughed when I blurted out, "I'm trying so hard to be patient."

"If you call that patient, I'd hate to see impatient," she said. "Come on Babe, you've got to give yourself a break. It's only been a month."

She was right, as she always is. (Man, I can't tell you how much that drives me nuts!) I needed to slow down, to take my time. I needed to accept that I didn't have to be productive every minute of every day. I needed to accept that the right job wouldn't necessarily appear right away.

And I needed to learn that whatever happens, however it happens, it's okay to walk (a little.)

I knew this on an intellectual plane, yet on an emotional level I was still grappling with feelings that were difficult to understand and articulate; that awful sense of being rootless and disoriented. No doubt much of it was a perfectly natural response; after six years in a singular environment, I was undergoing a predictable phase of dislocation, the consequence of a major change in my day-to-day routine and expectations. But there was something else I was grappling with, which could best be described as an existential sense of dislocation. Where was I going? Not just in my career, but in my life?

Seeking the answers to these questions partly explains how I found myself in this virtually unheard of place, a little dot on the North American map, thousands of miles from my home and my family. The other part of the explanation goes something like this; it was my wife's idea.

You may have already concluded that I am somewhat apprehensive about incurring Tanya's disapproval. To some degree, this would be a reasonably accurate assessment, although I presume this merely places me squarely in the middle of the vast majority of married men on this planet. It is prudent, however, to remind you that most men are not married to a woman who in a previous life was the leader of a herd of gazelles, or was nominated to run the final leg of the ancient Athens-to-Sparta postal delivery service. Tanya does not only cow me (one must be very judicious when using that term in the context of discussing one's wife) when running; she has also been known over the years to stridently express her dissatisfaction regarding numerous other areas of sub-par husband/father performance. So when Tanya felt I wasn't delivering according to the standards I committed to back in the heady days of our engagement (I wrote her so many soppy cards over a three-month period that I may have been personally responsible for the destruction of an Amazonian rainforest,) she saw it as her unflinching duty and noble responsibility to let me know.

Now any good husband will tell you that being reminded of your shortcomings by your loving spouse is all part of the natural cycle of love, life and marital longevity. What the less experienced will be aware of, however, is the importance of developing a unique kind of immunity to this feedback. This immunity plays an absolutely crucial role in developing the internal robustness to resist and deflect blatantly aggressive assaults on your character, ranging from; "As you did not stack the dishwasher properly, it's obvious that your first choice would have been to marry a maid"; to "I thought the story of the Grinch stealing Christmas was fictional until you came home from work today." So this immunity is not merely a tactic to deal with these attacks; rather it is crucial for a married man's survival. If you don't believe me, and if you're a male reading this, then just reflect for a moment on the term 'hen-pecked'.

There. I thought that would make it clear.

So what's this all got to do with me flooding the Swinomish River with my tears, especially as Tanya was thousands of miles away on the other side of the globe?

Some context here; even Tanya's good ideas, nor my fear of discounting them, don't simply result in my doing something as radical as boarding a nine-and-a-half hour flight bound for Vancouver, British Columbia, driving a hundred miles south across the Canadian border, and renting a little romantic hideaway for five days, especially without my wife. Actually, this good idea had its origins in Tanya's own career transition, which had occurred about six years earlier, coinciding with the time I joined the Bank. In some ways, hers was an even bigger shift than mine. She was emerging from ten years of full-time mothering to assume a major role in a not-for-profit organisation dedicated to promoting a unique approach towards mental health in the community. So instead of being a full-time mother, she was now a full-time mother with a demanding job.

Tanya and her colleagues teach and practise a form of psychology known as the Three Principles of Innate Health. Now admittedly I'm a bit biased here, but to my mind it's a revolutionary model that has the potential to seriously shift how we understand what constitutes a person's psychological well being. Understanding the three core principles – Mind, Consciousness and Thought – is crucial to making sense of our mental functioning; an appreciation which can lead to a much more serene and elegant navigation of the vicissitudes of life that confront us all.

George and Linda, a potent husband and wife team who are amongst the founders of this approach, have their base in this idyllic spot midway between Vancouver and Seattle. Tanya has been out here a few times herself over the years to further her own training, always returning from these trips spiritually and psychologically invigorated (though I reckon a few days away from the kids would have that effect anyhow, even if you were spending them in Broadmoor Prison.) Immersion in the understanding of these core Principles, both before and after formally working with them, has been crucial to her own emotional well-being and resilience. And it also led to a gap that began to emerge between the two of us. By that I do not mean a gap in intimacy, closeness or running ability. I mean that while she had continued to grow and deepen as a person, I had stagnated somewhat. So while her primary focus over the past six or so years had centred on her personal growth and evolution, mine had focussed on the need to advance myself and my earning potential at the Bank. Is the gap idea starting to make sense now?

Until now, I had always possessed what seemed a good excuse for not engaging in my own period of self-reflection and personal development amongst the pine trees and the geese; while SKBK Bank was more open than most institutions of its type, just imagine the conversation with my old boss; "Uh, Tony. I'm thinking of going to the middle of nowhere for a few days to explore my own innate sense of well-being and healthy mental functioning. But don't worry – I'll come back with a significantly increased capability for driving our syndication strategy and mitigating the risk on our latest securitisation transaction. So do you mind if I take that as paid leave?"

Now, I know what you're thinking. Why couldn't I have made the journey during my own time as part of my existing annual leave? Surely Tanya would be supportive, especially if it increased the likelihood that I would come back a nicer husband, a more tolerant father and bearing one of those 'I love Washington State T-shirts' she's always wanted. Well, this is where my excuse gets a bit thin. The truth is, sure I could have made the suggestion, and of course Tanya would have encouraged me – she'd probably have booked the ticket and driven me to the airport herself. But as I said, I had stagnated somewhat. The idea of self-reflection didn't really appeal. The thought of learning, listening and opening up didn't hold much attraction.

So I'd managed to avoid it thus far, citing work pressures, football match fixture congestion, and a surprisingly disappointing accumulation of British Airways miles as reasons for not being able to make the journey. But now, not working for the first time in sixteen years and in the midst of the football off-season, I was running out of excuses. Throw in the fact that I knew that if I suggested this trip, she'd be willing to forgo the new multi-speed, stainless steel fold-up treadmill for which she'd been saving in order to pay, and there was no option but to once again revert to my alpha male prototype and man up.

"Sweetie," I began in my most sycophantic voice. "How would you feel about me making a trip out to La Conner to do an intensive (five days of one-to-one counselling interspersed with personal reflection and slowing down time)? As I'm not working at the moment, it kind of makes sense for me to spend a few days out there getting a bit more self-reflective and all that. What do you think?"

Tanya looked at me as if I'd just offered to buy her Swarovski diamond earrings to wear to the FA Cup Final. This was definitely like all her Christmases coming at once, our Jewish faith notwithstanding. She composed herself sufficiently to avoid bursting into song, dance and prayer contemporaneously, and playing it cool, merely replied; "Great, I'll speak to Linda and set it up. When do you want to go?"

So there you have it. I had managed to make a complete hash of my redundancy. At a time when most guys in my position are expected to be out on the golf course or queuing up at Job Centres Plus, I was getting ready to embark on an extended process of self-development with some people I barely knew, in an unknown place on the other side of the world. It's one thing to be open, searching and willing to learn but maybe this was going a bit far (and I don't just mean geographically). It occurred to me that maybe losing my job was just the first step; was I also losing my mind?

But I'd made my bed and now I was going to have to lie in it...

July 4th

I looked across the simple wooden coffee table at Linda. A woman in her late sixties, she exuded a sense of peaceful calm and innate wisdom. Tucking a strand of slightly greying hair behind her ear, she focussed her thoughtful green eyes on me. Trying not to show my slight discomfort, I scanned the spacious consulting suite, thinking about how the simplicity of the room and its furnishings were entirely consistent with Linda's straight-forward, no-nonsense personality. She wasn't there to either impress or pressure. Her only agenda, as far as I could discern, was to listen, to reflect and to gently steer me towards the insights embedded within, that only I could discover and bring to life.

Yet that didn't make our conversation an easy one. The whirring of the overhead fan did little to liberate us both from the sweltering heat of her consulting room, and I soon felt the sweat beginning to trickle down the back of my neck and under my t-shirt. But the heat was not just coming from the outside. As insights began tumbling out of me while we talked, I felt on fire inside as well. And though there was pain in some of the self-realisations I was arriving at, buoyed by Linda's gentle yet firm reassurance, I ploughed ahead. For I had come here humbly, and wasn't about to let my ego get in the way now. We were talking about how I typically showed up in the world. And usually, if not always, it has been through the realm of my intellect.

Going all the way back to that IQ test when I was nine years old, my analytical mind had always been an important dimension of my cognitive make-up. Yet over the last six years since joining the Bank, it had taken on far greater significance - it had become my currency. This is not to suggest that I am some kind of brain-box who dazzled my colleagues with my brilliant ideas and creative input. Not by a long stretch. But it means that in order to succeed, in order to belong at that Executive table, I learnt to function in the realm of the intellect. I had convinced myself that what my parents and teachers had said over thirty years ago was true – that I belonged with the clever kids, and more significantly, that it mattered.

When he needed to find an approach to certain issues, Tony liked to tell people; "Discuss it with Brian. He's a smart guy; he'll work it out." That felt like a nice endorsement at the time, but in retrospect, it just compounded the problem. I was never the smartest guy in the room. But I was in and amongst them, thinking, analysing, strategising. I was paid to do that, but at what cost? The ego was being fed daily, yet it never seemed sated. The toughness and hardness had found a home, even if I did a good job of keeping it hidden from most people. Humility, gratitude, grace, openness – qualities which I had felt were innate parts of my emotional and spiritual makeup – had become sideshows in my quest to get to that table and remain there.

Becoming aware of this truth pointed me towards another; functioning primarily in the realm of the intellect has not been helpful to me; it has not served me well as a person, even if it outwardly benefitted me for a period of my career. That insight led me to acknowledge that what I always considered my greatest asset was becoming a liability. The importance I ascribed to the intellect was inhibiting me from connecting with myself, other people and the world in a far deeper, more authentic way.

"Somehow, I have neglected what it is like to feel, to be. I feel like I'm all caught up in my head, and not connected enough with my heart, my soul. There's a part of me that feels like it's gone missing and I can't seem to find it," I said softly to Linda.

"Yes, I've sensed that too," she replied after a moment's reflection. "It's what I like to think of as the soft, squishy Brian. And I really like him."

"That's right!" I blurted out. "Tanya calls it my vulnerable side. And she says it's a part of me that she loves so much, but that I keep hidden from her most of the time."

And then, as the potency of this understanding came pouring out of me, I began speaking with a startling clarity and conviction.

"I know it as the part of me that worries not about how I am being perceived or heard, but as the part of me that is authentic and natural and resonates with my own innate health. It is the part of me that when it surfaces, is in alignment with the deeper energy around me. It is the part of me that feels deeply, that connects with people, that immerses itself in relationship; that connects with the universe. It is the part of me that is soft, gentle and patient with my boys. It is the part of me that Tanya loves and craves to be with. And it is the part of me that connects with the Divine. It is the part of me that is spiritual. It is me."

Falling back into the soft, padded armchair, I felt spent. No therapy session had ever been as revealing for me as this. Across the coffee table, Linda remained quiet and still, gracefully allowing me to discover for myself what she already understood.

After a few quiet moments punctuated only by the distant cries of the seagulls circling the estuary, another thought broke through: "I've been so caught up in the future image of myself – what I should be doing, ought to be doing. I'm living for what I think my future should be. But I'm not living in the present, in the here and now. I'm so preoccupied with what it could look like that I'm not seeing what it is right now."

Linda looked at me with those deep, kind eyes, full of wisdom and patience. I shifted on my chair. The slight breeze blowing through the second-storey window wasn't enough to dissipate the intense heat. The sweat was dripping on my brow; the tears forming in my eyes. I tried to speak, but couldn't. I felt so alive with my own insight - Linda's profound offering to me.

Unusually for me, the silence between us felt appropriate. I sensed that I was experiencing the undiluted pleasure of slowing down, of deeply reflecting, of touching something deep within. So we both just sat there, not saying anything to each other, gratefully absorbing those feelings. And when the moment was right, Linda deftly nudged me towards one final, crucial understanding.

"I've got a name for that person who lives in the future image of himself," Linda said. "Let's call him Self Image Guy. He's the guy who sees what he should be, not what he is. He's the guy who operates in the world of the intellect – and does it pretty well. He's the guy who is always striving to achieve things – good things – in the world. He's the guy you've put a lot of energy into over the years, the guy you've spent a lot of time building up. He's the guy a part of you thinks you should be. And actually, in some ways, he's a pretty impressive guy. He's not a bad guy; he's just not you."

I sat silently, listening; really listening. Linda continued.

"There's another guy though, and he's the guy who is sitting in this room right here, right now. He's the guy who is not trying to go anywhere or do anything; he's the guy who just is. He's not trying to be anything; he's just being him. And because of that, he's a pretty special guy. I've got a name for him too; Regular Guy."

Linda's words resonated so strongly with every fibre of my being. And with this incredibly powerful insight came another wave of emotion that I could not contain. The realisation was so deep, so clear, so true to me that I couldn't help but weep. There was no other way to react to an understanding that could so profoundly change my life. In that moment, sitting in Linda's room, I became aware of what was paralysing me; of what was preventing me from living in a state of grace, calm and abundance. I had become so preoccupied with what I expected the life of Brian to look like, that I had forgotten just to be Brian.

It had taken a while but I had found the answer to the question Rabbi Dr. Katz had asked me back in London a couple of weeks before. I had finally come to understand that my self-image was what was holding me back. And amidst the tears, I somehow managed to smile to myself. It had been a very long time coming, but I think I was finally ready to start letting go of Self Image Guy. He could go back to Fessenden Primary School for clever kids. I preferred Regular Guy a lot more. And it was time to start getting to know that Guy better.

Sensing the lightness that had come over me, Linda smiled ever so gently. "And Regular Guy - that is the guy who feels connection with God."

I nodded. And we were both quiet.

July 7th

I have been to some beautiful places in the world, but the exquisite spot where I now find myself is as breathtaking as any I've ever known. A narrow strait sits between two mountains, creating an incredible natural phenomenon. Looking out to sea in either direction, one is confronted with the sheer expanse of the shimmering ocean, punctuated only by the multitude of small islands that characterise this pristine stretch of coastline. An enormous bridge was built in the early 1900's connecting the two islands and creating the soaring pass which thousands of cars use daily.

Today is the last of my five day intensive with Linda. I have come here this morning ahead of my final session before heading to the airport. Parking my rented Lincoln on the side of the road, I clamber over the railings, finding a gorgeous position where I can sit in solitude gazing out at this incredible spectacle. The early morning sun is radiant, bringing me warmth. My eyes water as I am overcome with the sheer beauty and vastness of the vista before me.

My mind wanders to the name of the place where I am sitting. It is called Deception Pass. How fitting. I have been deceiving myself for so long. It has been a good deception - so good that I didn't even know it most of the time.

Deception means intentionally to mislead someone. Had I intentionally mislead myself? Perhaps yes? Perhaps not? Does it matter? What really matters is the insight I had arrived at. I had become redundant. Not just from my job; from me. The gap between my self-image and my regular self seemed almost as large as the yawning chasm that separates the mountains on either side of the pass. The self-deception can no longer be ignored. Who am I: Regular Guy or Self Image Guy? And more importantly, which of those two guys do I really want to be?

The truth is that so many of the insights and understandings that have occurred to me over the past few weeks have been revisited here. I am seeing things more clearly than I can ever recall, both in sessions with Linda and during my own in-between periods of extensive reflection and solitude. More than anything else, my time here has created exactly that – time - as well as the mental, psychological and emotional space to slow down. My mind is used to working in overdrive – it has become so busy that it feels like it has been going at the pace of a Formula One engine. Problem is that the human mind is not designed to function at this level – not without ending up in a high speed crash or at least going into the workshop for a rest and tune-up, if you'll excuse the crude metaphor.

Once the initial breakthrough had taken place, it didn't take long for me to realise just how stuck I had become. Yes, I had been successful at my work; the redundancy had been a genuine one in that it was not about performance. The role had been discontinued, and therefore by extension, I was redundant to the organisation. I had already understood, accepted and moved on from that. But what I haven't moved on from is a much deeper, difficult to describe state of inner being. This has caused a lot of internal blockage. I have ground to a stop. I'm not talking about my career here - I'm talking about me.

Gazing out at the mass of endless translucent water, the metaphor of the marathon comes back to me again. I find myself thinking about what is required to build the capability to cover long distances: time, patience and expenditure of effort. In other words - miles on the road and under your belt. Memory needs to be built into the legs, and that only comes from extended long distance training – whatever the speed at which you're running – and as it builds, so does the capability to run increasingly further.

It occurs to me that perhaps this selfsame idea is true in life also. We all need to build our muscles – spiritually, psychologically and emotionally; we need 'hours on the road' to do so. But the paradox is inescapable; you do not and cannot, build capacity. It is innate. Which means that assuming the absence of a significant physical disability, every single one of us has the inherent capacity to run a marathon if we so choose.

On the five occasions when I've run the London Marathon, I've always been moved by the sight of the marvellously eclectic array of over 35,000 people participating in the same race. Fast and slow; young and very old; thin and obese; sighted and blind; famous and unknown; those in regular running gear and those dressed as enormous chocolate bars, superheroes, fairies, rhinoceroses, and all sorts of other crazy outfits. Novices and elite athletes 'compete' side by side. There are people of every background, ethnic origin, gender, education, social status, psychological makeup and physical characteristic imaginable. There are even some well documented cases of, for whatever reason, people taking up to a week to complete the 26 mile distance. There are virtually no exceptions. Even those in wheelchairs can and do compete (the same event; a different race.)

Yet my experience is that most people do not believe it is possible to participate in a marathon. Unless you are in the minority of regular long-distance runners, it seems too difficult, too out of reach, too beyond our abilities. In short, it seems impossible.

This is where good marketing people come in. Adidas plastered a slogan across the running shirt that every participant of the 2007 London Marathon received. (I know – I ran the race and I've got the t-shirt.) It read; *Impossible is Nothing*. In other words; it's not impossible to run a marathon; it just seems that way until you've achieved it. Then, once completed, you realise that the word impossible has nothing to do with it, therefore it is nothing. (My slightly more verbose explanation doesn't fit so well on a t-shirt; hence *Impossible is Nothing* works better and I'll stay away from applying for any marketing positions.) If you take innate capacity and add to that capability – which comes through training, developing muscle strength, increasing fitness, creating great running playlists, eating loads of carbs and all that good stuff – you become transformed into a marathon runner. Maybe not a Paula or a Mo, but at least you're in the same race.

Can the metaphor be extended? Can it be that we all have the same innate capacities; for well-being, for mental health, for self-insight, for self-regard? We may have different inherent capabilities – the physiology of each and every person is of course different, meaning that some are faster, some slower; some born with more natural stamina, some less so. And we may have developed and built those capabilities differently over time. But is it not possible that we all share a universal capacity for experiencing life with grace and equanimity? Could it be that this is not unique to particular people; that it is available to us all?

I have always thought of myself as the guy who managed change well; it was my life's script. I had lived on four continents, worked through some major life issues, changed jobs numerous times, undertaken significant career transitions. Not only had I specialised in change management in the bank, but I figure I was pretty good at in my personal life as well. Yet that was only true to a point. For when it came to deep, transformational inner change, I had simply lost the will. I had not just become stuck. I had become superfluous. Not to an organisation, but to myself.

But things have started to change over the last few weeks. The good news is that my five days with Linda in La Conner have given me the opportunity to reconnect with an old friend. Regular Guy has his faults, to be sure, but there is something about him that feels deeply familiar, and deeply reassuring. This makes perfect sense, for he is me. And with that insight comes a feeling so profoundly right, that I know with utter conviction that I am ready to return home; for I am not just ready to continue the search for another job. More than that, I am ready to continue the search for the deeper, more authentic, more regular me.

It's time to head back for my final session. I step gingerly back over the railings, padding over the soft ground as I make my way back to the car. Turning around for one last look at the magnificent view, I feel a deeply fulfilling sense of well-being envelope me. I can let go; I will let go. As I drive away from Deception Pass, I know that my deception has finally passed.

Half an hour later, I am back in Linda's consulting room. This session turns out to be much shorter than I expected, for there is not much left to say. We quietly talk through much of what I have learned, gently probing what it all meant and exploring how I can continue to reconnect with my deeper, more genuine self. And as we talk and our time together draws to a close, I realise I am feeling a more profound sense of inner calm and quiet than I have experienced in a very long time. I am ready to leave. It is time to go back to Tanya and the boys and a life that needs to be lived at least a little differently.

I know my journey is still at its very early stages, but at least I now have a sense of the path I am required to take and a glimpse of what a different future for myself might hold. Arriving at the airport terminal, I pull my boarding card out of my back pocket. It still has the name Brian Keith printed on it. And my passport picture hasn't changed much in the last five days. But this version of that traveller is beginning to morph ever so slowly into a different one. For if you look very closely, you may just be able to discern the very faintest of traces of a chap called Regular Guy making his way home.

12. Abundant

As we start to regain the relationship between our personal intelligence and our spiritual wisdom that lies within, we develop a higher degree of intelligence and common sense. This, in turn, clears up our misguided lives.
Sydney Banks, The Missing Link

August 4th
In my dream, I am back at the Bank.

There is a large meeting on the fifth floor which I am attending. Everything is obscured – only a few of the faces are familiar. I have the strangest sensation of having been away a long time; and yet not at all.

I feel uncomfortable being there; I don't really belong and I know it. So when the opportunity presents itself, I excuse myself and leave the room. I make my way to the lift, readying to exit the building, when I look down. I'm barefoot – no socks or shoes. Somehow, they've been left behind in the meeting room.

I'm terribly embarrassed, but cannot make my way home barefoot, so returning to the meeting room, I knock on the door. Without waiting for a reply, I stick my head in and ask the room full of people if they've seen my shoes.

"We had them sent to storage," says someone from Facilities. "You can retrieve them from there."

"Thanks," I mumble and retreat from the doorway, embarrassed and ashamed. I make my way out of the building quickly, hoping no-one will notice me. I don't look back.

When I awake, I am struck by the intensity of my dream. In spite of my earlier psychoanalytic training, I never try to make much sense of dreams – it feels almost like a dark art – but as I lie in bed, a thought occurs to me. In my tradition, shoes represent an interface between the physical and the spiritual realm. As the protector of the soles of the feet from the hard, unforgiving ground, the function of footwear is to ameliorate the physical world, making it more manageable and comfortable. Yet precisely because they perform a necessary function, shoes also inhibit connection to the higher worlds. In the famous biblical passage when Moses is asked to approach the burning bush, he is instructed to remove his shoes. The message; the spiritual pathway has no need for footwear.

Where have my shoes gone in my dream? How could I have left them behind in the building?

Perhaps my shoes were an obstacle, getting in my way. Perhaps they were preventing me from accessing an inner, more spiritual essence. Within the building, I required my shoes. But I exit the Bank without them, for they no longer serve any purpose; my needs have transcended them. In a spiritual world of abundance, shoes are unnecessary. Initially, I am embarrassed and ashamed. Exposed and vulnerable, the journey home will be uncomfortable, painful even. But I do not go looking for my shoes and I do not look back. I will find my way without them, for that way home has very different requirements.

The denouement of my story has remained unwritten for some time. I have grappled with how to approach its ending; what once seemed clear to me has become obscured? Why?

When I began writing, I had a clear pathway laid out in my mind; I would narrate my journey from superfluous to abundant, bringing with it a new perspective on the meaning of redundant and an understanding of all that I had encountered and explored; gratitude, humility, connection, sorrow, moving on, introspection, and self-understanding. All of which would lead to an inner state of abundance that would be the polar opposite of the painful feelings that had plagued me in the immediate aftermath of my redundancy.

Yet it has not been a straightforward track from one state to the other – at least not in the way I had expected it would. The real truth is that this abundant feeling is proving highly elusive. Just when it feels like I've got a grip on it, it pulls away. Just when I think I'm more or less there, something or someone pops up and seems to mock the very notion. Is abundant a mirage that I have been imagining? Is it a kind of literary device gone horribly wrong?

This is not to discount the plentiful gifts which enrich my life; six beautiful kids, an extraordinary wife, a wonderful and loving family. I have an amazing array of friends, guides, teachers, mentors and relationships. I have my faith, my values, my community. I may have lost a yard or two of pace but I still have my left foot and my undiminished love for the beautiful game. I have most of my hair, my health (if not my wealth), good shelter, acceptable clothing, and access to almost every technological device known to mankind. I have a soul that is readily touched, which can soar and connect to others and to the Source of all life. I have a heart that can feel love, pride, joy, sadness, empathy, hope and serenity. There is so little I lack and so much I have. Sure, I could do with a smaller mortgage and my own private study at home, but this would be quibbling. I am in need of nothing. My life is absolutely abundant, and I am deeply grateful.

But we've already established that a real state of abundance is something over and beyond that wonderful, inexhaustible list. It's an inner state of being, a place within the self. It's a state of mind which lives in a constant expression of grace and wisdom. It's that deep certainty telling us all will be well, that so much of what we desire and pursue matters not. It's that self-insight that sees through the illusion and connects us directly to our spiritual essence. It is a feeling so boundless and real and honest that it cannot be subjected to further enquiry or articulation. It's about God and Godliness, and the deep understanding that there really is nothing else.

And yet, still, I struggle. On the one hand, the feelings of peace and completeness are tantalisingly close. I have touched them before – atop Deception Pass, at moments of immersion in prayer, finding serenity in Linda's consulting room, with Tanya... On the other hand, I cannot hold onto them. They keep slipping away.

So now the self-doubts creep in. Whom have I been kidding? What kind of elaborate web of deception have I been weaving? I'm just an ordinary man trying to figure out his way, muddling through; some days good, others less so. As Linda said; I'm just a regular guy. Sure, my self-image has been holding me back, but I could say that about lots of things, couldn't I? An even more cynical thought occurs; I may have dealt with the job loss, but limitless feelings of abundance? Come on, it's time to get real here.

So what's it going to be? Superfluous or abundant? It can't be both. Or can it?

This has been the personal account of my journey. And I've come to realise that a journey by definition is never complete. It is not about an itinerary or reaching a specific destination. A journey is ongoing, perpetual, continual. There is no definitive ending. Its constancy and state of motion are what defines it. And not only is it far from complete; I now know that it can never be fully completed. I am here, as the great sages of my tradition taught, not to finish the task, but to participate fully and unconditionally in it.

My mistake was in thinking this would be a linear account, not in a chronological sense, but in a spiritual and psychological one. While I anticipated there would be a rollercoaster ride of tumbling emotions, I also assumed that as I moved through the intensity of despair and helplessness I felt on the very first night of my redundancy, I would gradually transition from a negative state of despondency to a positive one of abundance and contentment. I would have completed the voyage; arrived at my destination; achieved the sub-four hour target. End of story, end of book.

But I should have known better. For that is neither the way of journeys nor the way of the universe. And it is not my script; it is not me.

This insight is as important as any I've discovered. I am merely on a continuum. There will be moments and days and experiences when I am overcome by the blessings of my life and in the world around us. The universe will be perfect and I shall be grateful. And there will be other times when I might feel removed; when fears and anxieties threaten to derail me. I may feel disconnected, apart, detached, redundant. So I have now come to realise that it is not either one or the other; rather I must encompass both extremes, while I learn to navigate the journey with as much grace and wisdom as I can muster.

I have finally arrived at a profound conclusion; I will not feel complete and plentiful all the time; perhaps not even as often as I would like. But I will remain in a constant state of journeying. For abundance will always be available to me. It will always be available to us all.

And perhaps that is all we need to know.

There's one more story that needs telling, one that I've put off until now because of the emotional pain it evokes. It's been ten years, but the memories of fear, despair and sadness are so visceral that I can scarcely believe a decade has gone by since I received a call at work from Baruch, then only seven years old, one cold February morning.

"Daddy, Mommy says you must come home. She is feeling very sad and doesn't want to get out of bed."

I rushed home to find Tanya lying on the bed, at the end of her psychological tether. She had been struggling with post-natal depression and anxiety ever since Rafi's birth almost a year earlier. Tanya had always been prone to depression. Her struggles immediately following the miscarriage soon after we married would form part of the pattern she had lived with for much of her adult life. Mothering five young children and relocating to a country far from her natural support system exacerbated her sense of being overwhelmed and contributed to intense moments of emotional lowness. Having lived so long beneath the dark shadow of depression, Tanya was now staring into the abyss. Before we knew it, she was undergoing a real psychological breakdown. Tanya had hit rock-bottom; she felt she had reached the end, and could not carry on.

I wasn't sure I could either. My entire world felt like it was spinning on its axis. In that moment, as I looked down at the woman I loved so deeply, lying prostrate on the bed, I knew a desperation and fear unlike any I had ever encountered. I wanted to collapse there and then; to join her on the mattress; to hold her tightly and weep for what had brought her, had brought us, to this potentially catastrophic moment.

It was a luxury I couldn't afford. Instead, I had to hold myself together - for me, for Tanya, and for the kids, as we began the process of putting the pieces back together.

But to my surprise, something unexpected happened. We didn't need to put the pieces together. Tanya may have broken down for a while, but she wasn't broken. Confronted with a future filled with images of endless therapy sessions and psychiatric prescriptions, Tanya rebelled. She refused to accept what the psychiatrists said, what the literature documented, and what the conventional 'wisdom' in Western society expected her to believe; that she was clinically depressed; that she would probably need to spend the rest of her life (or at least a large portion of it) on medication; that she had an 'illness' that required acceptance, careful management and lots of outside help. This was nothing to be ashamed of, she was told; like millions of other people, Tanya suffered from depression, and probably always would.

But Tanya decided to write an alternative narrative to her story, one that would have a very different ending. She - no one else – decided that she was not psychologically ill. Tanya understood and accepted how much she had battled. She was not in denial. But crucially, Tanya began to see her psychological struggle for what it was; a very low state of mind born out of years of becoming habituated to thinking and feeling in a certain way. Tanya believed that things could be turned around; that she could delve into her own reservoir of innate well-being and take ultimate responsibility for her own psychological health.

And that is exactly what she did. Within a few months, and despite both my and the psychiatrist's strong objections, Tanya made the incredibly brave decision to discontinue taking all her medication. Not only did her mood begin to lift and her functionality increase exponentially, but she began to see life differently. Life hadn't become easier in a practical sense, but somehow it seemed to become lighter, an existence she wished to embrace, rather than one with which to constantly struggle. A fresh perspective emerged, one that Tanya infused with a grace and equanimity and a sense of joy and plenty. Enlightened is a strong word, but something about my wife was resonating with enlightenment. She didn't just become well; she became different, really different.

At first I thought it might simply be some kind of post-crisis high; except it didn't dissipate. As weeks became months, and months became years, the woman whom I had loved and lived alongside for the past ten years transformed before my very eyes. And the most remarkable thing is that she did it virtually on her own – with no medication and very little outside help. Nobody told her what to do or taught her how to do it. This was her own discovery, fuelled by a unique cocktail of drugs; self-insight, self-regard and genuine self-understanding. Tanya chose not to be defined by the self-image she had constructed and which she had continually re-enforced over the years. She no longer needed to be insecure and anxious, with accompanying feelings of inadequacy and low self-esteem. Instead, she could choose to be deeply happy with whom she was, discarding her emotional and psychological fragility and replacing it with a new-found resilience and sense of inner security. And she executed this transformation without ever losing the essence of her personality that I, and so many others, had fallen in love with. She was still the gentle, loving, exceedingly modest, humble, giving, caring and graceful woman she had always been.

I'm still not sure if I completely understand it, but Tanya's own remarkable journey to high functioning mental and spiritual health has taught me something invaluable. I have learnt from her what real abundance is, and perhaps more importantly, where to find it. She showed me that abundant is a state of mind and that it comes from within. It is not a quality that anyone can give you or even explicitly teach you. It must be self-generated, for that is the only authentic way in which it can truly exist and sustain itself.

Tanya's extraordinary and inspiring journey occurred ten years ago. I am a slower learner – I think that's often what happens when ego gets in the way. My fall had certainly been far less dramatic than hers, but the same principles applied. And now I needed to apply them to my life, to my situation.

You can only avoid the bleeding obvious for so long; my wife has become my ultimate guide in the journey from superfluous to abundance. She slew the self-image that served her so poorly for many years and replaced it with a perspective and understanding and lightness that was nothing short of transformational. I am not sure if I know of any other person who lives in such a state of abundance.

Inspired by Tanya's journey, I am now ready to continue to navigate my own.

13. Making sense of it all

Experience is not what happens to a man;
it is what a man does with what happens to him.
Aldous Huxley

August 15th
I am back in London. It is three months since Tony announced his resignation and set in motion the chain of events that changed my world so dramatically. We have just returned from a family holiday to Spain's Mediterranean coast. (Booked six months ago when money was more plentiful. It's a good thing I hadn't taken out holiday cancellation insurance, otherwise the kids would have ended up with a day's outing to Chessington World of Adventures instead of a week frolicking on the beaches of the Costa de Tropical.)

Basking in the Spanish sunshine, I had much time to reflect, perhaps too much time. Despite the dodgy wifi connection, I managed to access the Encarta Dictionary on my new version of Microsoft Word to research the term *redundant*. This popped up first: 'dismissal from employment because the job or the worker has been deemed no longer necessary.' So I find myself wondering: which is it, the job or the worker? When a person is deemed redundant by an organisation, is it because the job is no longer required? Or is it because the worker – in other words, a living, breathing human being - is declared no longer necessary?

I analyse this for a moment. The issues I have had to confront over the last few months - genuine concerns regarding finances, exploring future job opportunities, changes in domestic arrangements - and everything else involved in navigating the maze of unemployment have taken their toll. But challenging as it has been, I get it - at some point, one's job, role or task is no longer considered necessary – ergo, it becomes redundant. That doesn't mean this has been easy, but, and here's the key point, if I can accept that redundancy *is* about the role, if it *is* about the job, then by definition, it's *not* about the person.

On the other hand, if redundancy means that it is the *worker* who is no longer deemed necessary, where does that leave me? And herein, I am discovering, lies the core problem. I am aware of the need to separate the two elements - position and occupant - in order to preserve my sanity. Intellectually, I know redundancy *is* about the *role*, at least in a technical and legal sense it must be for an organisation to justify the decision in the first place. But let's get real here: no one who goes through the experience perceives it in such a binary, clear-cut manner; it is not merely one or the other. For I have no doubt that the vast majority – irrespective of what the HR professionals, employment lawyers, counsellors or career consultants say – internalise redundancy as a personal affront. All of which may seem counter-intuitive; it certainly runs contrary to the advice of many of the so-called experts. But they see only one side of the equation – the side that seeks to protect either the organisation, or the individual, or both, from as much harm as possible. It's a form of damage control. And though such an approach has merit, I believe that we do ourselves a great disservice if we ignore the personal, yet paradoxically universal, dimension of redundancy – the opportunity to take stock, to reflect, to engage in some genuine self-exploration.

Over the last three months, I have oscillated between extremes of sadness, hurt, anger, fear, anxiety and helplessness. My response has been to dig deep, regroup, begin the search for the next job and get on with my life. I have assumed that a different plan would emerge that I could single-mindedly pursue and make happen. In the immortal words of Hannibal Smith, the legendary leader of venerable 80's heroes the *A-Team*: "I love it when a plan comes together."

As a guy who has specialised in change, adaptation and just getting on with things, it was a plan that would have conformed to type. Yet had I blindly immersed myself in the next phase of my life, had I accepted that this was a merely a case of the role being made redundant and left the matter at that, I would have missed the point. I would have passed up a significant, perhaps once-in-a-lifetime opportunity, to generate some essential psychological and spiritual growth.

Being made redundant has been the catalyst for asking some troubling and searching questions; perhaps some of the toughest, most honest questions anyone can ask of themselves. What have I learned? How do I feel? What is the universe trying to teach me? What is holding me back? How have I lost my way? How can I find my way back? And underpinning all of these, one seminal question, the one I just couldn't seem to avoid: what does it mean to me, to you, to all of us, to *be* redundant?

My journey has taken me to some tough places and brought me face-to-face with some uncomfortable truths: I had become pre-occupied with my own success; I had become entrenched in ways of thinking about myself, my place in the world and my definition of responsible living; I had become attached to a self-image that was increasingly in conflict with my true self. But ultimately, though this is difficult to acknowledge, I am grateful. For had I not been forced into this situation, I wonder what would have become of me?

One of the perks of working at the Bank was the opportunity to attend a global conference every couple of years consisting of 600 senior people drawn from around the word. I say 'perk' because unlike some companies looking to cut costs during the recession years, SKBK decided *not* to relocate its most important international get together to the Greater Walsall region, Grimsby Town Hall or The Holiday Inn, Slough. Instead, as had been the case for the previous ten years, we were required by the Group Executive to take five full days out of the office, pack our goggles, flip-flops and Bermuda shorts and head for an all-expenses paid 'working' trip to the gorgeous, semi-tropical, sundrenched islands of the Seychelles. Some guys have all the luck.

For a small minority, the conference represented a highly stimulating opportunity to listen to a cast of outstanding guest speakers, ranging from Nobel Prize winners in Economics, to accomplished authors and global business leaders. For a large majority, the five day Seychelles excursion was a biannual occasion to drink copious amounts of free alcohol and learn critical new business skills such as scuba diving, snorkelling and flea market bargain-scouting. Alas, it was never easy to justify these trips to Tanya and the kids – but somehow, I always managed to find a way.

So there I was, ever so slightly hung-over, lying on my king-sized bed in a hotel suite larger than the downstairs of my house and dreaming about leading Team GB to the World Beach Coconut Volleyball Title, when the most peculiar noise began to intrude on my victory celebrations. Eventually stirring myself awake, I groped for my trusted friend, and upon locating the 'on' button, activated my Blackberry. 2:54 am. I closed my eyes and tried to return to the coconuts and white sand. But the unusual noise persisted in a strange, rhythmic way. As my senses began to clear and my head to pound, I realised that someone was desperately trying to open the door to my suite. The unmistakable sound of a hotel key-card being monotonously inserted and then reinserted wouldn't go away. Finally accepting that I wasn't going to lift the giant silver coconut trophy in this particular dream, I stumbled out of bed and opened the door. What greeted me, at 2:56 am in the doorway of my five-star luxury hotel room, was one of the most terrifying, shocking sights I have ever witnessed: a fully grown, frontally facing, completely stark, naked man.

I couldn't decide whether I should scream, call resort security or just accept that my dream had taken the most bizarre, surreal, nightmarish twist. Before I had time to properly contemplate these options, my survival instincts took over and I unceremoniously slammed the door in the face of the unwanted attempted intruder. Trying not to think about the frightening apparition I had just seen, I returned to my bed and closed my eyes. But moments later, I once again heard the repetitive and clumsy attempts to open my door. Naked Man just wouldn't go away. Knowing what to expect this time, I came prepared. Throwing the door open and turning my face 180 degrees so as not to have to bear witness to the full natural glory of my nocturnal 'guest', I flung the fancy towelling robe that had been hanging in the bathroom, hitting him square in his vacuously staring face. Then, with as much force as my semi-comatose mind could muster, I shouted: "Wrong room!" and slammed the door shut a second time. To my everlasting relief, Naked Man seemed to get the message and finally went away.

The next morning, seeking comfort following my harrowing experience, I mentioned my late night misadventures to a couple of colleagues over breakfast. By the time of the first mid-morning coffee break, it seemed as if the whole conference had heard about Brian and the naked man who tried to break into his room. Everyone from the Global CEO down seemingly found this the most hysterical event since the 2004 conference when Jim Saunders from the Sydney office fell fully clothed into the resort's main swimming pool while trying to sneak out of the key-note address being delivered by a former cabinet secretary. But, I was less inclined to see the humorous side. So seeking post-traumatic stress counselling (a verbose technical term for help), I went in search of one of my former OE colleagues who had a doctorate in Psychology.

First though, I had to navigate the mass of humanity descending upon the pastries and latte table, not to mention the extensive ribbing from fellow conference attendees, asking really amusing questions such as: "Hey, Brian, have you got a spare towelling robe for me?" Steeling myself, I eventually located Carol next to the mini croissants and Danishes. Steering her by the arm, I led us to the relative safety of the herbal tea station.

"Did you hear about what happened to me last night Carol?" I asked her naively.

"Sure Bri," she answered nonchalantly. "Everyone in the resort knows. I even heard two of the cleaning ladies giggling about it."

"That's great", I replied dejectedly. With today's instant communication, I had to accept that Tanya, thousands of miles away in London, had probably already heard about Brian and the Naked Man. I was going to have some explaining to do when I got home.

"Thanks for the reassurance Carol. Anyhow, I wanted to ask you what that whole thing was all about last night. I mean, how do you make sense of some strange naked guy with a vacant stare trying repeatedly to enter my room with the wrong key in the middle of the night? Jokes aside, it was actually pretty disturbing. Surely, even if he was really drunk or something, he'd have realised the first time when I slammed the door in his face that he had the wrong room? So what was going on?"

"Oh, that's easy to explain." Carol replied matter-of-factly, her voice taking on the tone of the expert in psychology that she is. "That guy, whoever he was, was sleep-walking. That's the reason he kept trying to slot the key-card in the holder outside your room, and it also explains why he didn't react when you first refused him entry. My guess is that it was only when you hit him with the towelling robe (she'd already heard about that; it's uncanny how fast the details of this story had spread), that he jolted awake and realised he was trying to get into in the wrong room."

I spent a moment absorbing Carol's interpretation of events, and, concluding that she was spot on, thanked her profusely. "That explanation really makes sense Carol. At least I know now that there isn't some naked man on the resort stalking me in the wee hours of the morning. I think I'll be able to sleep better tonight knowing that."

Carol gracefully accepted my thanks, though as I wheeled away and tried to grab the last custard tart off the table, I'm sure I could hear her snickering.

This ridiculous recollection returns to me now. Somehow, almost in spite of myself, I feel a kindred spirit with my naked, nocturnal visitor from that strange night on an island resort. While I may be fully clothed, I too feel as if I have been sleep-walking through the last few months. It has been a strange, surreal kind of dream. One day I was on the fast-track to success; the next day, suddenly and without warning, I was out of a job. And now that I've awoken, and accepted what *has* happened to me, that I have been made redundant, that I have left the Bank and am never going back, I am left trying to make sense of it all.

When I stepped onto the platform of Bank station at the beginning of September, 2007, I was placing my foot on the first rung of a new ladder. I was carving out a radically different career. I was convinced that I needed to open doors to the world of business and high finance if I were to lead the life I had persuaded myself was worth living. Steered by the invisible hand of my own hyped-up self-image, to which I soon became unknowingly enslaved, I then pursued my own success relentlessly, if not ruthlessly. The toll it took on my authentic self and the way I aspired to be in the world was rarely obvious to most people, but those who knew me best – my wife, children and dog come foremost to mind – could see it. I was still a reasonably good guy; I just wasn't the guy I used to be. Hubris had become my constant companion; attachment to my version of achievement my ally; ambition my greatest vice. I had lost my true self, and I was struggling even to acknowledge it, never mind seeking a way back. So while striving and advancing in the financial epicentre of the world that is the City of London may have been serving Brian the city banker, it was no longer serving Brian the human, spiritual being that I am. Nothing could be more revealing than this understanding.

While redundancy *has* forced me to re-assess and re-balance, I have also come to realise that there are aspects of my fundamental character - my drive, energy, calm temperament, desire to contribute, and aspiration to succeed – which will always be there. And be there they should, for these qualities constitute who I am, and always will. Knowing that, I continue the search for the right work environment, within which these dimensions of myself can be valued; where I can flourish and make a contribution, and where I can continue to authentically develop and evolve as a person.

So many other precious insights and lessons would contribute to my personal growth. I learnt from many guides and mentors who came forward at the right juncture, some of whom I'd known for over twenty-five years, others for a fraction of that time. They joined forces with events and memories to create a potent new energy. And thus, I learnt about the fickleness of life from Tony, Craig, Rupert and whomever else had an influence, either advertently or inadvertently, on the discontinuation of my role. I learnt that I should have listened, really listened, to the automotive voice of the London Underground, warning me to "mind the gap." I learnt what it felt like to feel helpless in the face of events beyond my control. I learnt about the power of the corporation and the loneliness of the individual, who, when push came to shove, could be discarded, set aside, rendered surplus. I learnt the cathartic power of opening up to my own grief. I learnt from a good friend about the importance of letting go and how difficult that could be. I learnt about the dangers of self-importance, and the damaging effect of being overly attached to one's own success. I learnt about the need to ground my ego – especially for the sake of my children, and the pitfalls of unbridled ambition.

I recalled the lesson I'd learnt years before about letting go of resentment towards my father, and applied that understanding to my departure from the Bank. In the same way I was able, over time, to forgive my Dad, so too could I forgive those who played their part in the sudden decisions that brought about my redundancy. I learnt, from a wild idea of running a car washing business, about the possibilities available to me if I could only open up to a universe that is always interconnected and meaningful. I reflected on the gap between being religious and being spiritual, and appreciated that a genuine experience of spirituality need not be so elusive. And I learnt that no matter how strange you look, nothing is too odd for Brighton Pier. I remembered the utter terror and helplessness I felt when lost in the African bush at night, and the immense gratitude I felt when I was rescued. I learnt that I could re-engage the soft, gentle, open side of myself that is so important for my relationship with my family. And in so doing, I came to more deeply appreciate the imperfect perfection of the six wonderful boys that Tanya and I have co-created.

I was grateful for the numbers of people – both at work and beyond – who cared about me, offering genuine support, heartfelt empathy and practical assistance in lifting barbells – both literally and metaphorically - off my chest. I learnt about humility, and how that could facilitate a deepening of perspective. I learnt there's a time when simply walking is the right thing to do; that manically pursuing the next achievement at breakneck speed is not always the best or most likely way to achieve a desired outcome. I learnt about the journey from superfluous to abundance; that it is not a linear progression, but rather a route with many twists and turns. And I learnt from my remarkable wife, the greatest of all my teachers, about the true meaning of abundant – of a life lived in a state of fullness and grace and plenty.

And finally, I learnt that no matter how many lists I made, there is no substitute for the most simple, obvious questions, like the crucial one asked of me: "What's holding you back?"

I learnt from Linda, more than any other, about the corrosive and insidious consequences of my inflated self-image. She helped me to see that I had become a slave to it, and, crucially, to understand that it was an illusory belief out of alignment with my true self. And so, I *did* learn what was holding me back. Most importantly, I learnt about somebody whom I'd long forgotten, somebody who got left behind when I joined the school for the clever kids, somebody called Regular Guy.

Of course, my experiences, my trials, my journey, are mine and mine alone. You will have your own challenges and your own journey. For we can never fully know or understand the other; at best, we can learn from each other. And if my story has helped you understand and learn something about your own story, then we will have achieved something meaningful together, something that transcends our personal stories and becomes far more universal and far more binding for us all.

In late November, 2000, I found myself looking through tear-filled eyes at what is undoubtedly the biggest graveyard in the world. Has there ever been a single location in history where more people have been murdered in cold blood than the three million human beings killed by the Nazis at the infamous death camp known as Auschwitz-Birkenau?

I cannot think of any single experience in my life that has helped me to generate perspective more than those brief hours standing in the biting wind, gazing incredulously at burnt out crematoria, endless rows of killing fields and the sheer scale and enormity of the nightmare scene of brutal, systematic murder that presaged the attempted annihilation of an entire people. This was the place where mankind descended into greater mass depravity than perhaps any other time in history; a place so immersed in pernicious, unimaginable wickedness that its very name will forever be associated with terms such as the Holocaust and genocide.

Walking through what remains of the mass murder factory that was Auschwitz-Birkenau, looking upon a single enormous room filled with nothing but piles of children's shoes so numerous that it becomes completely impossible to fathom, let alone count them, a single, overwhelming question permeated my consciousness: How do I make sense of this?

And I quickly realised that nobody would be able to offer an answer to this most unanswerable of questions. Nobody would be able to offer me understanding. All I could do was to ensure that I did not look away, no matter how uncomfortable it was. I could absorb, bear witness, and, to the degree that was possible, reflect on what could be learnt from an experience that however painful, I would not shirk from.

One of the many effects of that first, briefest of trips to Auschwitz, was to put so much else into perspective. I would never be able to make sense of what had occurred in those gas chambers. But I also came to realise that I didn't need to, for sometimes all we have is our faith to guide us when the rational mind no longer can find its bearings.

And in the starkest of contrasts, it implied to me that there is so much else in my life that I *could* make sense of, assuming I was willing to keep asking the questions and searching for the answers. Perhaps not perfect sense, for that would be attempting to claim some kind of enlightenment which is certainly beyond me. But I have no doubt, and have never doubted, that there are lessons to be learned, messages to be absorbed, insights to be generated and, crucially, changes to be made based on all that I have experienced. This has been the fundamental principle underpinning the telling of the story of my redundancy. For if I do not strive to make sense of it all, if I do not strive to learn from all that I have experienced, I would have failed myself. I need not find out all of the answers, but I must never shirk the responsibility of asking all of the questions. And in so doing, the sense of it all, of uncovering this great, mysterious tapestry called life, will slowly begin to reveal itself ever more.

And as I *have* begun to make sense of this all, I have arrived at an understanding of myself radically different from that of a few short weeks back. I have learned that to be *made* redundant is not to *be* redundant. The former was an event imposed upon me, over which I had little control. The latter is a state of mind that I could choose – that I *do* choose – to discard on my voyage of self-discovery. Therein lies the great gift that redundancy has given me.

What happens next, I do not yet know. All I know is that I must remain committed to the journey ongoing, for therein lies the humility, perspective and understanding that will sustain me. In the meantime, I am deeply comforted by this single thought: I may not yet have found the right job. But I think I may have found me.

Epilogue

God doesn't play dice with the universe
Albert Einstein

Have you ever felt, when you stop to reflect on your life, that there is a pathway unfolding, and that if you're just willing to be sufficiently patient and open, sooner or later it will all become clear?

Today, almost five months since I was made redundant, I started a new job. Except that it's really an old job - sort of. I have come full circle, back to where I started in the UK almost fifteen years ago. I have returned to the not-for-profit organisation which employed me before heading to the City. They were looking for a Chief Operating Officer, someone who understood the group's culture and mission, but who could also bring industry experience and corporate know-how. I guess I'm that someone.

Had you said to me just over six years ago that I would land a great job at a top tier bank in the City of London; I would have laughed at you. Had you told me six months ago that I would be made redundant suddenly; I wouldn't have believed you. And had you told me six weeks ago that I would come back to work with the same organisation and wonderful people with whom I started this whole journey, I would have politely suggested you were crazy. But all of that is exactly what has happened. I really have come full circle. And perhaps that is the final lesson I needed to learn from this stage of my life; to surrender, to truly let go, to be completely open to the unfathomable ways of the universe.

That universe has always had its plans for Brian Keith. Now, more than ever, the pathway has become illuminated, its ways clear. I feel so grateful to have been given a glimpse of what they are. The rest is up to me.

October 16th, 2013
London

Acknowledgements

I am grateful to the many people who have played their part in this book's journey. Their feedback, honesty, guidance and encouragement have been critical.

Lionel's enduring patience and belief in the story I wanted to tell has never wavered. And thank you Marc for making the connection.

Many past colleagues played their part. You know who you are and how you contributed. Thank you.

I am privileged to work currently (and many years back) with an extraordinary team of people: dedicated, selfless and exceptionally talented, led by one of the most committed, passionate and spiritually focussed people I have ever known. Thank you all at JFT.

I have been deeply impacted and taught by what has often felt like an almost limitless supply of guides and teachers, not all of whom are still with us. Many of you are mentioned within these pages in some way or another; some are not. The truly great ones are also the most humble.

My in-laws, and Dan, have been unstinting in their support. Mom's contribution to this book was immense, not to mention a whole lot of other things which only mothers know they do for their children.

The Boys are everything and though I say it too infrequently, I am immensely proud of them.

At our wedding, I referred to the biblical verse that expresses how 'the splendour and beauty of the king's daughter is contained within,' related to my new wife's extraordinary qualities. Almost twenty years later, that understanding has proven to be truer than ever. How fortunate am I.

I thank God daily, though almost always not as meaningfully as I would like, for the countless blessings in my life.